Like and unlike
Stages 1, 2 & 3

A Unit for teachers

D1489269

Published for the Schools Council by
Macdonald Educational, London and New York

© Schools Council Publications 1973

First impression 1973
Second impression (with amendments) 1975

ISBN 0 356 04350 9

Published by
Macdonald Educational
49-50 Poland Street
London W1

850 Seventh Avenue
New York 10019

The chief author of this book is:

Albert James   Deputy Project Director

The other members of the Science 5/13 team are:

Len Ennever   Project Director

Wynne Harlen   Evaluator

Sheila Parker
Don Radford
Roy Richards
Mary Horn

Made and printed by Waterlow (Dunstable) Limited

General preface

'Science 5/13' is a Project sponsored jointly by the Schools Council, the Nuffield Foundation and the Scottish Education Department, and based at the University of Bristol School of Education. It aims at helping teachers to help children between the ages of five and thirteen years to learn science through first-hand experience using a variety of methods.

The Project produces books that comprise Units dealing with subject areas in which children are likely to conduct investigations. Some of these Units are supported by books of background information. The Units are linked by objectives that the Project team hopes children will attain through their work. The aims of the Project are explained in a general guide for teachers called *With objectives in mind,* which contains the Project's guide to Objectives for children learning science, reprinted at the back of each Unit.

Acknowledgements

The Project is deeply grateful to its many friends:
to the local education authorities who have helped us
work in their areas, to those of their staff who, acting as
area representatives, have borne the heavy brunt of
administering our trials, and to the teachers, heads and
wardens who have been generous without stint in
working with their children on our materials. The books
we have written drew substance from the work they did
for us, and it was through their critical appraisal that our
materials reached their present form. For guidance, we
had our sponsors, our Consultative Committee and, for
support, in all our working, the University of Bristol.
To all of them we acknowledge our many debts: their
help has been invaluable.

Metrication

This has given us a great deal to think about. We have
been given much good advice by well-informed friends,
and we have consulted many reports by learned bodies.
Following the advice and the reports wherever possible
we have expressed quantities in metric units with
Imperial units afterwards in square brackets if it seemed
useful to state them so.

There are, however, some cases to which the
recommendations are difficult to apply. For instance we
have difficulty with units such as miles per hour (which
has statutory force in this country) and with some
Imperial units that are still in current use for common
commodities and, as far as we know, liable to remain so
for some time. In these cases we have tried to use our
common sense, and, in order to make statements that
are both accurate and helpful to teachers we have
quoted Imperial measures followed by the approximate
metric equivalent in square brackets if it seemed sensible
to give them.

Where we have quoted statements made by children, or
given illustrations that are children's work we have left
unaltered the units in which the children worked—in
any case some of these units were arbitrary.

Contents

Introduction

The need to sort things

'She can recognise my voice' explained the mother of a three-month-old baby who, while being held by an admiring group of women at one side of the room, was vigorously trying to turn her head over her shoulder towards the place where mother was chatting to someone else.

All of us live and learn simply because we are endowed with senses by means of which we are able to perceive the properties and behaviours of things. Perception leads to discrimination: we look for differences between things and likenesses between things in order to classify them. Young children do this almost instinctively and find it interesting. The ways they use for grouping and classifying their collections are very many indeed. They vary according to individual interests and the needs of the moment.

Later, as experience grows, arranging objects, behaviours or ideas into sets having properties in common, helps us to store and use more easily the knowledge we have gathered and also gives us an effective background framework against which we can match up new and novel observations. We find that there are certain accepted classifications which are widely used and worth learning about, such as those for the road system of the country, for the books in a library, for plants and animals or for the chemical elements.

Different people may have very different degrees of ability in the use of their senses to observe facts and relationships but everyone has this ability in some measure from the start of life and it is one which teachers must care about developing. They might look for the following in their children:

1. Development of powers of observation.

2. Development of an ability to sort out and to group observations in a variety of ways in order to help solve particular problems or to make decisions.

3. Some learning about ways of classifying and how useful they have been in extending knowledge.

At first, fairly rough and general observations may suffice but later the use of measurement and controlled experiment will be called for and aids for the senses will be needed.

The arrangement of this Unit

In all the Science 5/13 Units, work automatically involves observation, sorting out and grouping in order to study such things as small animals, structures, materials or even holes. In this particular Unit an attempt is made to pick out a thread of thinking for its own sake.

As a result, the Unit has an orderly sequence about it which some teachers might be interested to follow, but, on the whole, it is most likely that as work with children proceeds, groups will arrive at springing-off points into other areas of exciting activity most profitable to explore. For example, the use of a $\times 20$ microscope, here considered simply as an extension of our senses, will without doubt start some children off on an extensive study of small animals. For these valuable excursions in depth many teachers will feel the need for more detailed help and will find it fairly readily available in other Science 5/13 Units (*Minibeasts* in the case of the example quoted), in Nuffield Combined Science, Nuffield Secondary Science and Nuffield O-Level texts.

There are two chapters (Chapters 2 and 4), which are written particularly to consider branching out possibilities, mainly with a view to suggesting topics which more advanced children might follow up, perhaps while others are moving more slowly. Chapter 5 comes back to the main line of *Like and unlike* again.

The over-all aim is to introduce ideas in which unhurried practical experience, thought and discussion at a simple level will be both good and complete in themselves and also of value in helping children to a basis of understanding for the more systematic science teaching which may follow.

This Unit differs from others in that Stages 1, 2 and 3* are considered together in the one book. Often it will be possible to deal briefly and quickly with Stages 1 and 2 as there is a great deal of material already available in other Units and to move fairly rapidly to suggestions for work suitable for children reaching Stage 3.

See page 68 for definitions.

Plan of the Unit

1. Properties of things

   2. Branch lines
3. Using the senses
   4. Aids for our senses
5. Sorting out
6. Differences which form a sequence
7. Separating things
8. What use is all this?
9. What about Objectives?
10. Apparatus and materials

A refinery where the constituent parts of oil are separated

Sorting in everyday life

3

1 Properties of things

Contrasting pairs

The simplest activity is to make collections

The simplest activity is to make collections and lists of objects arranged in two sets with contrasting properties. Some examples would be:

Heavy	Light
Smooth	Rough
Symmetrical	Non-symmetrical
Tough	Brittle
Nice smell	Nasty smell
Bright coloured	Dull coloured
Attracted by magnet	Not attracted by magnet
Sweet	Sour
Rounded	Having sharp corners
Feel warm	Do not feel warm
'Bendy'	Rigid
Shiny	Dull
Float in water	Sink in water
Dissolve in water	Do not dissolve in water
Waterproof	Not waterproof
Conduct electricity (from battery)	Do not conduct electricity

Enjoyment comes from being imaginative both in selecting the contrasting properties and in looking for interesting objects to include in the collections, not simply a few obvious ones. A teacher needs to give only a few ideas for a start and then children should choose their own contrasting properties and set up their own exhibitions. Sometimes they like to set up two groups without labels to make others guess what the contrasting properties are, often making the answer far from obvious.

Working outside
Take care not to restrict the collections to objects which can be placed on a table. It is important to go out and use the outside environment too. Here one can contrast big and small (eg a tree and a moss, a double-decker bus and a mini-car); sunny and shady; fast and slow (eg an aeroplane and a snail); walking birds and hopping birds; noise and pleasant sounds; sheltered places and exposed places and very many more. All in all, out-of-doors observations often produce much more stimulating results than those from the often somewhat contrived materials brought into a classroom. It was interesting to notice in the trials of the

Water

Waterproof or not?

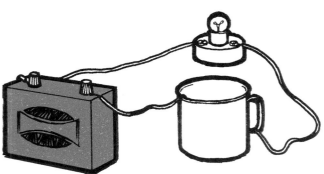

Conductor of electricity or not?

Unit the difference in involvement between some children who made up their circuit for testing conductors and insulators and took it outside to test everything they could find, including manhole covers and many parts of teacher's car and another group who were given the work to do as a set 'experiment' with only a few test objects on a table.

Using books
Of course we must use books. It would be silly not to include the elephant and the whale in a list of large animals because we were unable to visit a zoo or take a voyage to the Antarctic. However, it is almost always the opposite state of affairs that seems to need guarding against, ie the use of pictures and books almost to the exclusion of first-hand observation of the wealth of things which surrounds us.

Comparing more than two properties

It quickly becomes apparent that a simple division into two sets is generally too crude. Some objects we have do not fit either category. At this stage we can have a 'don't know' or 'not sure' section or make collections having more than two sections, for example:

Transparent, translucent, opaque.
Rigid, 'bendy' (elastic), plastic.
Nice smell, nasty smell, no smell.
Animals covered with skin, fur, feathers, scales, something else (eg chitin of beetles and other insects).
Round stems, square stems, triangular stems, oval stems.

Children will, no doubt, soon come up with a group of objects in sets such as:

Smooth leaves, hairy leaves, simple leaves, compound leaves (ie made up of separate leaflets like rose leaves), prickly leaves, stinging leaves, leaves with smooth edges, leaves with serrated edges.

This should lead to some discussion and perhaps to the realisation that one often has sets which overlap.

Overlapping sets

There are sub-sets which may also overlap.

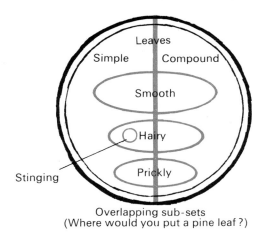

Overlapping sub-sets
(Where would you put a pine leaf?)

One ten-year-old boy who was interested in music produced the following diagram.

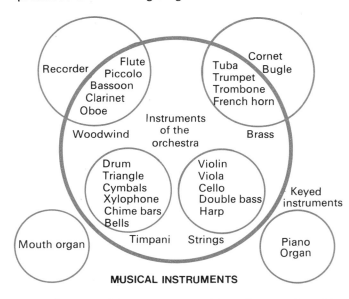

MUSICAL INSTRUMENTS

There is no useful purpose served in going too far with this. Find a few more overlapping sets but remember that it is all too easy to bring into consideration too many properties and so cause confusion. Remember that the sole reason for any classification or diagram is to *simplify*. The idea is taken up again in Chapter 5.

Sequences

Often there will be no sharp divisions to be noticed at all but a graded sequence, for example:

A set of blocks of different kinds of wood, all with the same measurements can be arranged in order of weight or hardness. The same can be done for a set of equal-sized strips of metal. In this case one might also arrange the strips in order of 'bendability'. (More advanced children can think if there are any more sequences, eg the order in which the polished metals tarnish.)

A set of leaves could be arranged in ascending order of area. This activity can be given several degrees of difficulty. It can, for example, take quite an amount of work to decide whether a lupin leaf or an ash leaf has the bigger area.

A series of sheets of different materials (eg paper, cloth, plastics, glass—each of several kinds and thicknesses) could be ranged in order from transparent to opaque.

How many polythene bags in a pile will still let light through?

What light are you going to use for the test?

Does the answer differ for different kinds of polythene bag? (eg what about the 'tissue' bag?)

Through how many polythene bags can you see someone at a distance of 2 m?

The colours of the rainbow make an interesting sequence. A group of children could also make a range of *tones* of colours (a tone is the hue plus white) while another group could build up a sequence of *shades* (a shade is the hue plus black). Then some interesting paintings could be done using tones and shades as well as raw hues.

This idea of properties arranged in an ordered sequence is taken up again in Chapter 6.

2 Branch lines

Some directions which might be taken

The last chapter was concerned with quite elementary activities in grouping things according to chosen properties. In the discussions which are bound to take place, the opportunity will arise for teachers to start off many projects which they may have in mind at a more advanced level for those children who are able to go further.

The following examples might be a guide to a few developments of this kind although there are many other possibilities. No attempt will be made to deal exhaustively with any topic, as teachers will find much help in other Science 5/13 Units and elsewhere. The intention is to indicate some useful directions in which one or more groups might take off.

Measuring areas, volumes, weight
Almost all collections (eg woods, metals, plastics, stones, bricks, bottles) lead inevitably to the need to measure lengths, areas, volumes and weights.

Lengths and areas
Lengths and areas of regular objects will not be difficult for children at this stage. There are many problems which are more interesting.

How are you going to find the area of a sycamore leaf or the part of your foot which presses on the ground when you walk? Is it a different area which touches the ground when you run?

One infants class found some interesting things about this by painting feet with thickly mixed powder paint and walking or running along a strip of spare wallpaper.

A junior class found that dusty feet after a PE class made quite satisfactory prints. They even found some good toe-prints and did some work to discover if everyone's big toe made a different print in the same way as finger-prints differ. (See page 39.)

How are you going to find the area of a curved surface (eg a ball, a bottle, a car door, a telephone, yourself)?

Volume
Volume seems to be a difficult concept to many and early work on comparing the capacity of boxes, cans and bottles of all kinds both from figures stamped on them and by comparing the amount of water or sand needed to fill them, needs plenty of time. Even the older children seem not to have gathered clearly the concept of conservation of volume if they have had little concrete experience. It is worth spending time on such activities as looking at 1 litre of water in different-shaped bottles, and measuring out volumes of water equal to the capacity of the engines of well-known cars, setting these out in order in a row of labelled buckets.

What about the volume of a model car or other irregular solid? This is quite a difficult problem. A common way of solving it that several groups of children have thought of, is to surround the model with clay and then to cut away the clay along a median line. If the clay is allowed to harden, the volume of the two depressions can be found by filling them with water. Most ten-to-eleven-year-olds were pleased with this method, though not happy about lack of accuracy. Several groups got rather widely different results for the volume of the same model. They were all pleased when their teacher came up with a better way. They could find out how much water the model car pushed out of place.

Displacement cans of different sizes are easy to make.

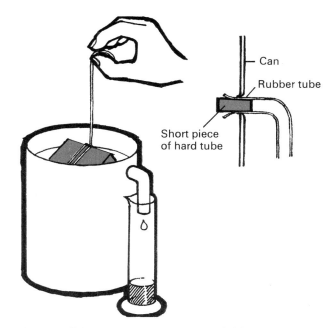

Can

Rubber tube

Short piece
of hard tube

A large nail is knocked into the can fairly near to the
top to make as neat a hole as possible. Into the hole is
forced some rubber tubing of such a diameter that it
makes a very tight fit. The apparatus may be good
enough at this point if there are no leaks, but if there
are, try a little clay around the join or, better still,
improve the fit by forcing a short length of hard plastics
or metal tube inside the rubber one as shown in the
drawing.

The can is filled to overflowing with water. When
dripping from the tube has stopped, the object whose
volume is needed is gently lowered into the water, and
the overflow caught and measured in a measuring
cylinder (plastics ones are good for this stage).

The operation itself is enjoyable so long as it is not just
a matter of recording figures. There are plenty of
interesting questions to solve. The children who were
trying to find the volume of the toy car liked this
method better than their original one. The displacement
can method gave very consistent results too but they
were puzzled by the fact that the volume seemed very
much less than before. They thought out the reason
after a while. They were now measuring the volume of

metal in the toy, while before they had been measuring
the volume of the interior in addition. To see if they
were right, they filled the inside of the toy with
Plasticine before finding its volume in the displacement
can and got almost the same result as they had done
at first. They went on to compare the amount of metal
needed to make various models.

Here are some further questions:

Can you find how much plastics or glass is used to make
different bottles?

What is the volume of your hand or a pair of spectacles?

What could we do with objects which *float?*

What about objects too big to go in any normal can,
like a bicycle wheel? (The answer to this one must wait
until the concept of buoyancy can be used, see
page 12.)

Can you find the volume of air sent out by one stroke
of a pump or a balloon inflator?

When you use an inflator to blow up a balloon, does the
volume of the balloon equal the volume of air blown in
by the pump? If not, why not?

When you find out the volume of anything how
are you going to know whether your answer is
right?

How *accurate* is your answer?

Several groups will have to work at a problem
independently and then compare answers. Any answer
very much out of line with the majority can be thrown
out and the average of the rest obtained, remembering
that it is no good giving this average more accurately
than the results warrant. For example if measurements of
a volume are recorded by different people as 20 ml,
18 ml, 210 ml and 21 ml we may obviously leave out
the 210 ml reading and take the average of the others.
It is no use giving this as 19·66 ml because no
measurement was made to less than 1 ml. A fair result
would be 20 ml and we must also remember that this
might be at least 1 ml out either way.

If possible, several different methods of working should be used as well. We have already seen how useful this was in finding the volume of the toy car. The question about the volume of air blown out of a pump was also tackled in two ways. The first method was simply to measure the pump barrel and use mathematics. The second method is shown in the drawing.

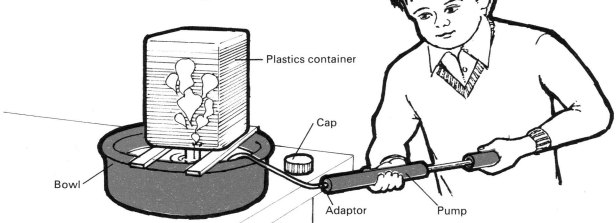

Plastics container

Cap

Bowl

Adaptor

Pump

The plastics container is filled with water to start with and the cap put on. When it has been inverted in the bowl of water the cap is removed and one pumpful of air blown into it to push out some of the water. The cap is replaced, the container brought right way up on to a table and the amount of water needed to fill it up again is measured. How near are the two answers? How near would you expect them to be? How near do your results agree with those of others? How many times has it been done? What is a fair average?

Weight
Weighing will be an important occupation. Children may invent and make weighing machines for themselves. These usually involve stretching elastic or springs, or bending metal strips, eg hacksaw blades. (See 'Force measurers' in the Unit *Structures and forces Stage 3*.) Other balances will work on the lever and pivot principle. These compare masses and do not 'weigh' strictly speaking. There will be a need for a good quick-reading balance to weigh up to 1000 g with an accuracy of 1 g. (See Chapter 10.)

Nuffield O-Level Physics texts and Nuffield Combined Science texts describe a very useful and simple drinking-straw balance for small weights. This is illustrated on the next page.

Some skill is needed to construct it and several straws should be tried to get just the right proportions and balance. A scoop shape is cut in one end of the straw to provide both a pointer and a place to put the object being weighed. The needle is inserted just above the axis of the straw and 2–5 cm from the end. It rests on two hard horizontal edges, eg of a piece of metal channelling. Choose a screw which fits the tube tightly. This is screwed in or out to get the correct balance. The scale may be marked off arbitrarily or calibrated using weights which are fractions of a gram.

Can you weigh a pin? . . . one mustard seed? . . . one square centimetre of paper? . . . a daisy petal?

In all the work, try to avoid weighing objects just for the sake of the exercise. There are plenty of questions which give a little more challenge.

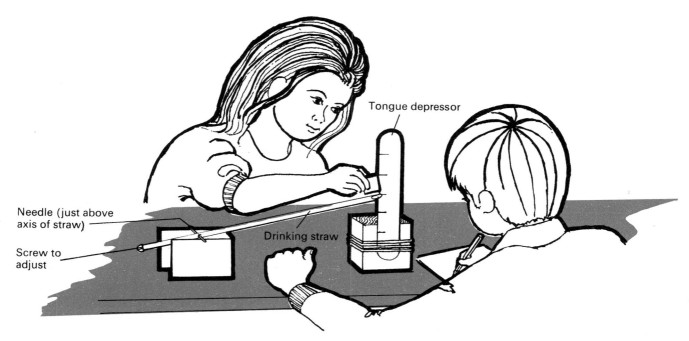

Needle (just above axis of straw)

Screw to adjust

Tongue depressor

Drinking straw

Can you find your teacher's weight if you have no balance which will weigh more than 1 kg (eg kitchen scales)?

How would you weigh the milk in a bottle?

If you hadn't got a drinking-straw balance, how could you estimate the weight of a mustard seed?

Look at some poppy seeds. They are very small indeed. Could you work out a technique for estimating the weight of one of these?

Is it possible to weigh the writing on a piece of paper? Weigh a length of pencil lead. What would be the shortest length you could weigh on your most sensitive balance? How much writing do you have to do to use up that length?

Does Biro writing weigh more than pencil writing? Weigh a full Biro tube and an empty one? What length (and hence weight) of ink is used up for a page of writing? What will you have to do if one page of writing doesn't use up sufficient ink to be measurable?

Density

If one sees to it that there are sets of different materials all having the same volume (eg blocks of different woods, pieces of different metals or plastics) or if one places side by side exactly similar-sized blocks of expanded polystyrene, balsa wood, oak and clay, for example, it is easy to see that the same volumes of different stuffs have different weights. Materials have different *densities*.

We can *compare* the densities by weighing equal blocks. We can give a *figure* for the density of anything by saying how many grams per millilitre it weighs.

What is the density of Plasticine?

Could you find the density of cooking oil?

One junior class found that a blue engineering brick weighed more than a common house brick. One group argued that it was made of heavier stuff, another that the house brick had a frog (hollow) in it and the other hadn't, so that made the difference. How would you settle the argument?

Buoyancy

Children have probably played 'floating and sinking' since infant days. Don't be boring; have some interesting problems.

Do conkers float? . . . india rubbers? . . . coke? . . . a candle?

Do all kinds of wood float? (Try to include ebony and/or lignum vitae.) Are all woods equally good floaters?

Do all stones sink? (Include a piece of pumice stone.)

Do seeds float?

Do all empty bottles (with stoppers) float? (Include empty scent bottles.)

To make things float the water must be pushing those things upwards. Push down a block of balsa wood or expanded polystyrene floating in a bowl of water and *feel* the upthrust. The water pushes up on everything in it. Try the experiment as shown on page 13 (top).

How much does the water push up?

For things which float, it pushes up exactly as much as the weight of the thing. For things which sink, it pushes up less than the weight. Next do the same experiment with a displacement can, page 13 (bottom).

How many millilitres of water does the object push out of place?

How much does this water weigh?

(You will find it easy to say how much the water weighs if you remember that the gram was chosen in the first place as the weight of 1 ml of water, but it might be as well actually to weigh some water to be clear about it.)

What general thing do you notice about the results of the experiment?

Try the same experiment with several more objects to see if 'it always works'.

Does Plasticine float? Try a ball of it. Next mould it to make a thin bowl or boat-shape and try again. Does the Plasticine weigh the same now? What makes the difference? Try the Plasticine in a displacement can in each of its two shapes. What do you notice about the volume of water displaced? Without using a balance, say how much the Plasticine weighs.

The upthrust on an object in water depends on the amount of water displaced. It is equal to the *weight* of water displaced.

Why does a steel ship float?

Could you now answer the question on page 9 about finding the volume of a bicycle wheel? You would need to take it to a pond or a swimming pool along with a spring balance.

Electricity

When sorting out some contrasting properties (page 5) we set up a circuit for selecting conductors and insulators. Is this test really *fair*? Might there not be some 'in-between' things? Try a piece of coke and a pencil lead (graphite, a form of carbon).

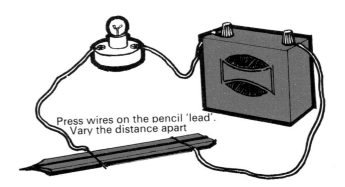

Press wires on the pencil 'lead'. Vary the distance apart

Vary the distance apart of the contacts. With the pencil lead you can start by pressing the ends of the wires on to the lead fairly near together and then sliding them apart. What happens?

It helps to prevent the lead from breaking if the pencil is split leaving half the wood as shown.

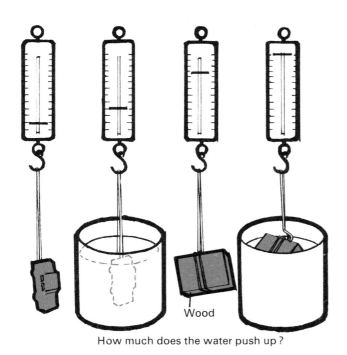

How much does the water push up?

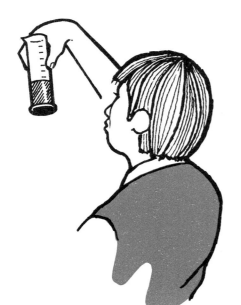

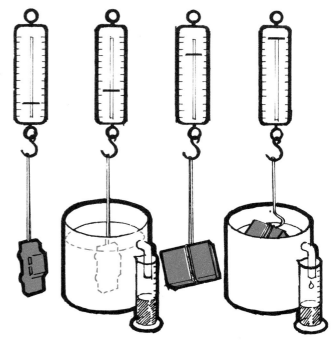

How much does the displaced water weigh?

When the contacts are wider apart there is more *resistance* to the current.

Is water a conductor or an insulator? Try the circuit shown in the drawing.

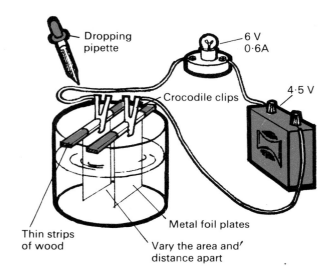

Dropping pipette

6 V
0·6A

Crocodile clips

4·5 V

Thin strips of wood

Metal foil plates

Vary the area and' distance apart

Cut the foil from one of the plates or dishes that pies are sold on, rather than cooking foil which is too thin.

When all is connected, drop dilute acid into the water from a bulb pipette (medicine dropper), counting the drops. Hydrochloric acid or sulphuric acid (accumulator acid) may be used.

What happens?

Watch the surface of the metal foil carefully.
Starting with pure water again try stirring in some salt, a little at a time. If the bulb shows that a current flows, vary the distance apart of the two pieces of foil.

Change the area of the plates. What difference does this make?

So it appears that you cannot divide things absolutely into conductors and insulators. In any case, we have only tried electricity at a pressure of 4·5 volts.

Suppose we double or treble the pressure by using two or three batteries as shown.

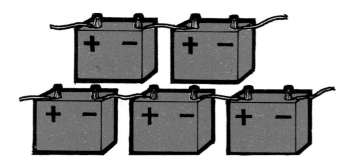

Beware. Let no one be tempted to use the mains.
The human body is quite.a good insulator at low voltages but a reasonably good conductor at high voltages and **mains voltage is dangerous.**

Take the things you have classified as *insulators* and *poor conductors* and work with these. *Don't* try the good conductors with more than one battery or you will simply blow the bulb.

Even if the bulb does not light up at all, how do you know that some small current is not flowing? The current could be insufficient to make the filament glow. Is there a more sensitive current detector than a bulb? Try making the simple one shown.

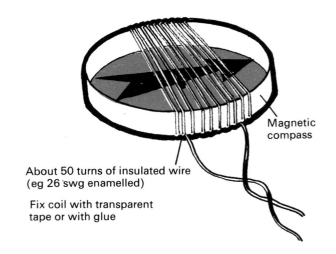

Magnetic compass

About 50 turns of insulated wire (eg 26 swg enamelled)

Fix coil with transparent tape or with glue

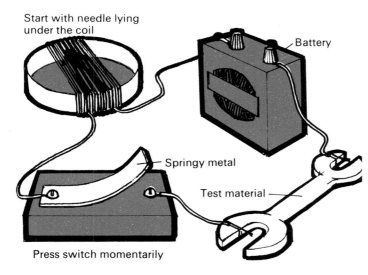

Start with needle lying under the coil

Battery

Springy metal

Test material

Press switch momentarily

What is the effect of altering the number of turns of wire around the compass?

If it is found to be difficult to wind the wire directly on to the compass, use a matchbox tray or similar small box as shown below:

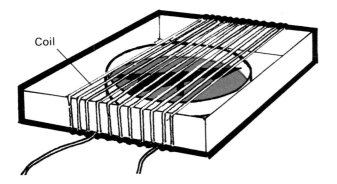

Coil

When in use, always arrange the position of the compass so that the needle lies parallel to the coil of wire to start with. Even a tiny current, eg from an almost completely 'run-down' battery, will cause the needle to kick.

Can you invent other current detectors? What is the best design?

What is the weakest salt solution through which you can detect a current from, say, a 1·5-V battery with plates 3 cm apart? How did you record the strength of the solution? What is the longest distance you can pass a current through a line of pieces of coke (pressed together) and still detect it?

Our starting point of 'like and unlike' (conductors and insulators) is already taking us a long way, but if interest continues on electricity, work on circuits, batteries and electromagnets could very well follow. These things are dealt with in several other Units (*Early experiences, Metals Stages 1 and 2, Science from toys Stages 1 and 2*).

Light and colour
From the starting point of comparing colours, tones and shades (page 7) a group might well set out to extract colours from petals, berries, red cabbage and other plants in order to make paint or dye cloth. They would find a great deal of interest in the Unit, *Coloured things Stages 1 and 2*. Collecting transparent, translucent and opaque sets may lead to an interest in light, for example reflection by smooth surfaces and scattering by rough surfaces or particles.

Lenses or prisms included in any of the collections (for example, of shapes or materials) would start work on refraction of light and colour.

3 Using the senses

Another good way of starting early work on comparing the properties of things is to consider how we make use of our five senses to do it. (See also the Unit *Ourselves.*)

Things we can tell by touching

Blindfolded children may be asked in turn to record all the things they can find out about collections of objects using the sense of touch. Lifting and general handling is allowed as well as simple touching.

Other children should build up many collections and should be encouraged to include objects in order to solve particular questions.

Can one distinguish between orange peel, lemon peel and grapefruit peel?

Can one distinguish between grades of sandpaper?

Can one distinguish between sandpaper and emery paper?

How does the sense of touch vary between different people?

Can one get more sensitive results by touching objects on the forearm or the cheek rather than by using the finger-tips?

A tape recorder is an excellent recording device for this activity. The actual words used by the blindfolded child can be played back for the whole group to discuss. Confidence, hesitation and searchings for the *right* word and phrase are all revealed.

Observations such as the following will no doubt be made.

Texture
For example: rough, smooth, greasy, waxy, furry, carved, moulded, ridged, angled, crumbly, sharp, prickly.

Shape, size and weight
Some children will be able to guess linear measurements and weights. Guessing volumes (eg of jugs, pans, bottles) seems very difficult. Names of regular shapes like cube, pyramid, sphere could be learned but irregular shapes are much more fun!

Is the weight evenly distributed?

Does the object topple easily?

Will it balance?

Where is the centre of gravity?

Check on all the guesses when everyone has had a go.

Structure
Is the object jointed or in one piece?

How is it put together?

Do some parts move? What kind of movement?

Temperature
Objects, especially metal ones, could be warmed on radiators or cooled in a refrigerator or outside before each test. One could introduce expanded polystyrene and wool which *seem* to be warmer. Are they really?

Can you arrange dishes of water in order of temperature from cold to hot?

Dampness

How sensitive is our touch to tell dampness?

Is it just that damp things usually feel cold as well?

Arrange a line of similar pieces of cotton cloth or blotting paper. From a bulb pipette (medicine dropper) drop 5, 10, 15, 20, etc, spots of water on to the pieces in an even pattern and wait for them to spread.

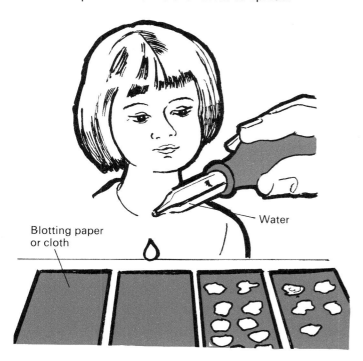

Water

Blotting paper
or cloth

Can you distinguish different degrees of dampness by touch only? Try to arrange the pieces in order of dampness while blindfolded.

Hardness

A set of objects such as putty, modelling clay, rubber, balsa wood, oak, lead, aluminium, steel, a soft sandstone, chalk, limestone, granite, could be tested by pressing, twisting or scratching with the thumbnail and a pen-knife.

Fragile or tough?

A cream-cracker, an egg-shell, a thin sheet of balsa wood, a sheet of very thin plywood, a piece of card, a sheet of aluminium, tin-plate or brass, would be interesting to compare.

Teachers are often glad to use the opportunity this work provides to help the children build up a useful vocabulary. It is surprising how much information can be obtained from touch alone. Blindfolded children can usually identify many materials: wood, metal, plastics, glass (**care no sharp edges**), pottery and even different *kinds* of cloth. They will immediately announce 'This is Plasticine', 'This is a conker', 'This is a piece of bark' or 'This is a toy car—a model of a Jaguar.' Much of this facility has been built up, of course, from previous experience of seeing and touching at the same time.

Things we can tell by smelling

It is usually easy to decide whether something has a pleasant smell, an unpleasant smell or no smell at all. Lists may be made from everyday experience. (The smell of 'fish and chips' seems to have the highest rating with many children.)

Other interesting lists to compare would be 'smells in the country' and 'smells in the city.' Fewer children will be familiar with the former (horses, cows, pigs, sheep, goats, poultry, corn, cattle food, silage, molasses, manure, artificial fertilisers, tractors, new-mown hay); many more will know the latter (diesel fumes, petrol fumes, smoke, drains, a polluted river, the hairdresser's salon, the supermarket, inside a bus, the swimming bath).

A great many common household things may be set out in small containers with lids to be identified by smell alone.

A good list would be:

Coffee, tea, flour, soap, detergents, moth balls, shoe polish, various spices, apple, pear, banana, orange, lemon, cheese, fish, smoked bacon, kippers, onion, carrot, parsnip, cabbage, potato, turnip, currants.

In addition there are a number of common liquids:

Vinegar, turpentine, paraffin, cooking oil, several disinfectants and antiseptics, shampoos, cleaners containing ammonia, lemon juice, lime juice, Coca-Cola.

Take care—use small quantities, ie one or two drops in a tube, **never** ammonia solution on its own or any such thing as Harpic, dry cleaning fluid or petrol.

Can you identify newspapers and magazines by the different smells of the printer's inks which are used?

The garden provides many smells to investigate in a similar way. Flowers and herbs such as rose, lavender, rosemary, mint, thyme and sage are obvious but don't forget that children often know the less familiar scents of dandelions, lupins, phlox, pansies, marigolds, nasturtiums—delights which adults may have forgotten. Remember too the subtle scent of hay, straw and damp soil.

An interesting thing about the sense of smell is that it seems very useful in warning us about *changes*, eg an escape of gas, the souring of milk, the rotting of eggs, fish, meat or fruit.

Some children may be able to observe a dog closely for some time to see just how much it makes use of a sense of smell.

Things we can tell by tasting

Great care is needed here about *what* is tasted and about cleanliness. This care needs teaching to children as much as care on the road and this might be a good place to do it. Children should be taught never to taste anything not known to them or checked by a responsible adult. There are especial dangers in berries, seeds, fungi, tablets and other medicines, cleaning fluids and other 'chemicals'. In the following experiments on taste then, there should be proper teacher control, very clean containers and disposable spoons, lollipop sticks or drinking straws to use for each test.

(If the standards imposed here produce discussion of

the hygiene in, say, motorway cafes or the way the cutlery is handled for school dinners, so much the better.)

How many of the following can you identify when blindfolded?

Apple, pear, banana, grape, onion, potato ,coffee, cheese, chocolate, vinegar, lemon juice, lime juice, soda water, salt, sugar.

Can you group them into sour, salty and sweet sets?

Does it make any difference to the results if you hold your nose so that you can't *smell*? (Potato, onion, apple and turnip would be quite difficult to separate.)

Can you tell what fruit flavour a wine gum is supposed to be if someone else pops it in your mouth when your eyes are closed? Try this with different-flavoured jellies too.

One group of children decided to make some jelly by mixing four different flavours in order to find which was the dominant one. This was in order to check their results from simple tasting tests, when they discovered that there was one flavour which was recognised by everyone and many indefinite ones.

Another, older, group found that even when most tastes could be recognised, different children took different times to do it. They produced interesting graphs comparing the times taken.

Can you tell the difference between butter and margarine? What is a fair test? Is one try enough? Is one kind of butter and one kind of margarine enough? Would it be a good idea to have a whole range of butters and one margarine or a whole range of margarines and one butter? One margarine has a percentage of butter in it. Can you pick that one out? How are you going to record the results?

Can you distinguish between sugar and saccharine? Again, how are you going to devise a fair test?

What is the weakest salt solution, orange squash, lemon or lime juice you can taste? How do you measure the

amount used ? Show the amounts on charts. A teaspoon-
ful in a litre of water in a kitchen measuring jug is a
useful starting point. If half the solution is poured away
and fresh water added to make up the litre, then one is
halving the concentration each time.

For all the activities, can you find out how different
children in a group have different ability to taste ?

In both smelling and tasting experiments it should be
possible, and very interesting, to compare children with
adults and in some cases, smoking adults with non-
smokers.

Things we can tell by listening

Be quite still and listen for two whole minutes. If possible
run a tape recorder at the same time, but if you haven't
one, write down all the sounds you hear. What do the
sounds tell you ?

Collect recordings or lists from many different places.
Everyone in a class could do a different one. One can
choose from an enormous number of places; in a playground, in a busy street, in a wood, in a supermarket,
in a church, in a bedroom, in a discotheque or by a
waterfall.

A teacher could produce recordings as puzzles in
identification (either identification of a specific sound or
of the place in which the recording of a mixture of
sounds was made). One class was puzzled for a long
time by a recording of the sound of their own lunch time.

How good is your hearing ?

How far away can you hear a pin drop ?

Does it matter what height it is dropped from or what
surface it drops on ?

Does it matter which way you are facing ?

How far away can you hear a particular clock ticking ?

Can you find out if each of your ears is equally good ?

How are you going to devise fair tests ?

Many schools seemed to find that young children can
generally hear better than adults. Is this true ?

Play any two notes at a time on a piano, chime bars or
xylophone. Which sound pleasant together ? Which don't ?

Get an empty bottle and tap it to make a sound.
Gradually fill it with water, tapping as you do so. What
happens to the note ?

Get someone to play different musical instruments
somewhere where you can't see them (or listen to a
recording). How many can you recognise ? It is an even
more difficult test to try to identify a sound made in any
way at all. Can you, for example, recognise a ruler
'twanged' on the edge of a desk, a cup tapped with a
pencil or cloth being torn ?

How many common bird songs can you recognise ?
Gramophone records are a great help with this. (See
Chapter 10.)

Can you recognise people's voices ? One child may be
blindfolded while others repeat the same sentence in
their normal voices to see if they are recognised. Some
teachers have tried recording each child on a tape and
then, by playing back to the whole class, finding how
many voices can be recognised. The children seemed to
find it easy to recognise almost everyone except
themselves, which interested them very much.

Things we can tell by seeing

Sight is the sense we use more than any other. How well
do you see ? A torch lens may be covered with black
paper with a pin-hole in the centre. How far away can
you detect that the lamp is on ? What difference does it
make if you do the experiment in sunlight, on a dull day,
at night, in a dim corridor or a blacked-out room ? Try
each eye separately. Do different people produce
different results ?

Letters about 5 or 6 cm high may be cut out of black
paper and mounted on a white background. How far

away can you read them? Start a long distance away and move nearer until you can just make them out. Compare different people. How do you make the test fair? As well as having several sets of letters so that the person being tested cannot *remember* them, don't forget to have equally good light conditions each time and to do the test several times. See that the letters used really are of standard size and shape and are always spaced in the same way.

Are white letters on a black background seen equally well?

What about white letters on a blue background (motorway signs)?

Are capitals or lower-case letters of the same size easier to distinguish or is there no difference?

Try to find which colour combinations are good ones to use for signs and which are bad ones. Have you tried purple letters on black or yellow letters on white?

It is all very well being able to see acutely but how well do we notice and observe?

Try taking a group for a very short walk and see how many observations can be written down on their return.

Try showing ten objects for a few seconds and see how many can be remembered after they are removed from sight.

Do you improve with practice?

All together

Normally we use our senses in combination and relate the sensations together in our memory. Having seen and touched the bark of a tree, we can later recall what a similar bark feels like just by looking at it. By looking at a can we are able to imagine the sound it would make if tapped with a pencil or the taste of what is inside it. We can even hear music in our head by looking at notes written on paper, or people's voices as we read their letters to us.

Which senses do we use to know about the wind, a damp wood, a city street, bonfire night, a birthday cake?

4 Taking it further: aids for our senses

For those children who are able to do more advanced work than the simple activities on the use of our senses which have been suggested in Chapter 3 there are many interesting ways of development.

Our senses alone are not good enough to take us far. We need to extend their range. We need to see further, to see smaller things, to see more detail. We need to measure more accurately, to measure things moving very quickly or very slowly, to measure the universe at one end of the scale and the atom at the other. We need to detect happenings and qualities such as radio waves which our senses will not by themselves detect at all.

The more advanced children in a group would need to spend little time on Chapter 3 and could very profitably move on to the use of some instruments and equipment. There should of course be a *reason* for using them, if possible an open-ended problem to solve. Very often the nature of the activity could be exactly the same as for Stages 1 and 2 except that it requires measurements too accurate for our unaided senses or observations which cannot be made using our senses alone. The following are a few ideas. Notes on apparatus will be found in Chapter 10.

Hand-lenses ×8 or ×10

There ought to be plenty of these available. In fact until there are plenty and they are freely used it might be as well to postpone getting more expensive magnifying equipment. Hand-lenses open up a new world *when used correctly*.

Use a good light. Hold the lens *near the eye*.

Bring the object up to the lens until it is in focus or move the eye and lens *together* nearer to the object. In other words, use the lens as an additional part of your eye and never separate the two.

Look at parts of flowers (don't miss grass flowers in June) ; the stings of a nettle ; skin ; hairs ; paper ; cloth ; small animals' legs, wings, antennae, mouthparts, markings ; powders ; crystals.

The possibilities are almost unlimited. For example, one might investigate the points of things such as pencils, felt pens, pins and needles, or the edges of things such as papers, cloths, leaves or knives.

Good light

Move this hand to focus, not the lens

This would be a good place to look at Robert Hooke's drawings of the edge of a razor and the point of a needle and perhaps read of some of the other things he did and the early history of microscopy. (See 'Books', Chapter 10.)

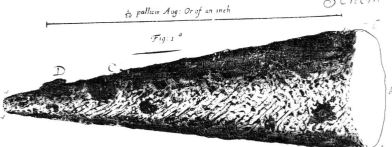

Robert Hooke's drawing of the point of a needle

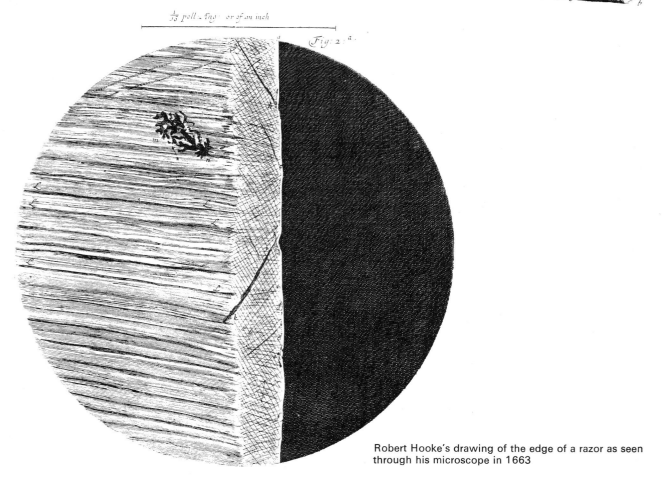

Robert Hooke's drawing of the edge of a razor as seen through his microscope in 1663

A simple ×15 or ×20 microscope

This should be one with adequate depth of focus and *not* made specially for viewing slides by transmitted light. (See Chapter 10.) Using it enables one to carry further the kind of interests which arise from using a hand lens. Again good illumination is important. It can be used for detecting *small* differences, eg in stamens of flowers, the antennae of woodlice, the weave of different pieces of cloth, the design of postage stamps, the hairs of human beings and/or pets, the leg joints of water beetles, the wings of flies.

Do spare time for simple delight in looking at a good magnified image, especially if your microscope is a binocular one so that one can see three-dimensionally. Try such things as small fungi, lichens, a coloured feather, a butterfly's wing or a dragonfly's eye.

How much does it magnify?

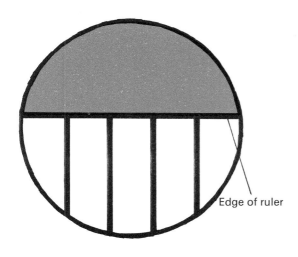

Field of view = 5 mm diameter

Make a drawing of something you see under the microscope. How many times bigger have you drawn it? Have a guess.

Now put a ruler on the stage of your microscope and see how many millimetre divisions appear across the whole diameter of the field of view.

Then about how many millimetres across was the object you drew?

Now measure your drawing. How much is it magnified? How good was your guess? Suppose it is magnified 52 times, we should write ×52 by the side of it. When you make your drawings like this, always remember to write on the magnification.

Look at some microphotographs. There are two on pages 24 and 25. You will sometimes find a different way of marking magnification. A line is drawn with the symbol μm over it (μ is a Greek letter pronounced 'mu'). One μm = one millionth of a metre and the line shows how long this length has become in the picture. One μm is often called a *micron.* Children may be able to picture its size better if they think of it as one thousandth of a millimetre.

About how many times has the picture on page 25 been magnified?

Rulers, calipers and micrometers

How accurately can we measure with a wooden ruler?

Is a steel ruler any better?

Look at wood, plastics and steel rulers under your ×20 microscope. How well and accurately are they made? Compare new rulers with battered ones.

Measure the width of a piece of paper with each of them.

One Teachers' Centre checked as many makes of metre rules as they could buy and found remarkable differences in their lengths.

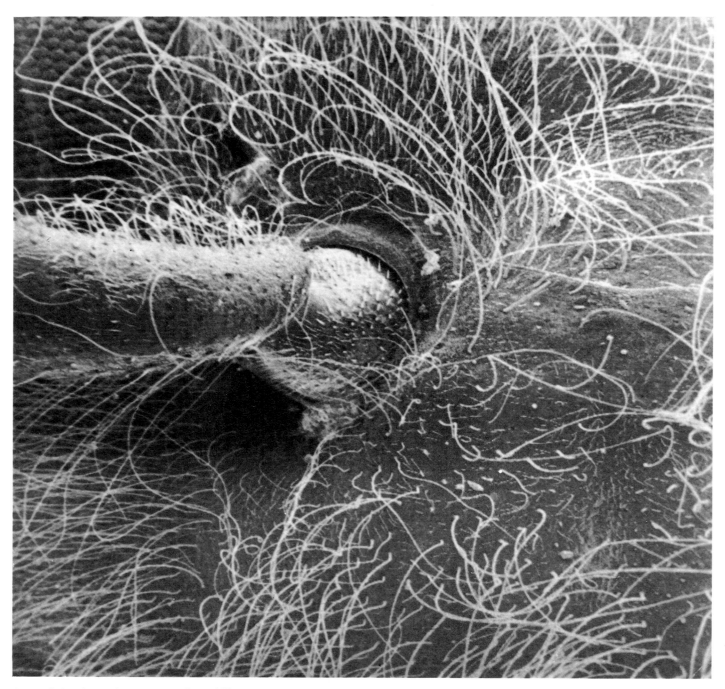

A wasp's head showing sensor socket x 122

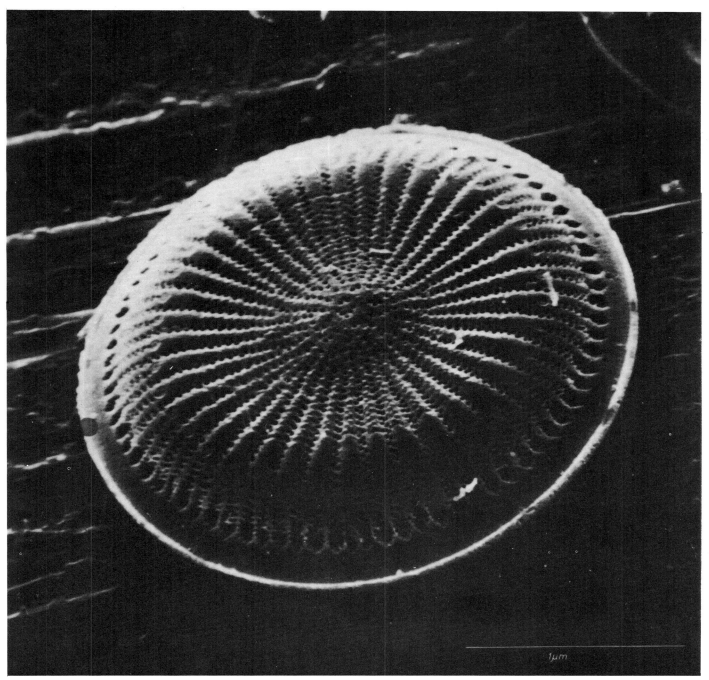

Auckland diatom

A very simple caliper is easily made from two pieces of card and a ruler.

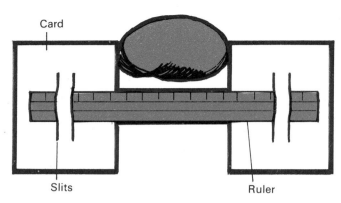

Card

Slits

Ruler

Make some larger ones for measuring trees or the size of heads.

If the cards are shaped like those in the next drawing, the inside diameters of tubes, necks of bottles, etc, can be measured.

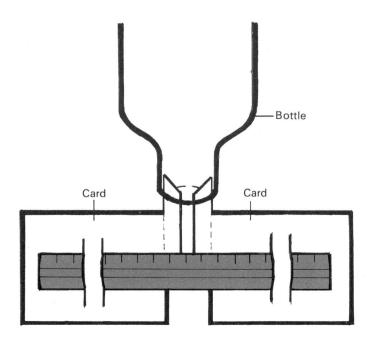

Bottle

Card

Card

There are some useful plastics models of calipers and micrometers in the Osmiroid measuring set. (See Chapter 10.)

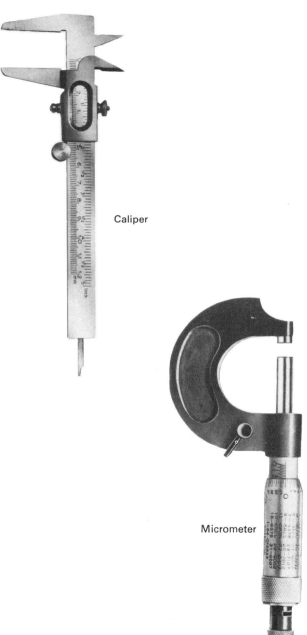

Caliper

Micrometer

Don't try to explain Vernier scales at this stage but it is reasonably easy to *use* them with a little practice and some children may be able to use calipers such as those shown to measure the amount of wear on bicycle tyres or brake blocks.

Use a micrometer to measure the diameter of different wires, hairs, ball-bearings, etc, and the thicknesses of sheets of different kinds of metal, plastics, card and paper.

How accurate is a micrometer? They too are useful for measuring *wear*.

Try to get worn disc-brake pads or piston rings from a garage and compare them with new ones.

Binoculars or telescope

Few schools have them but they may often be borrowed. One can sort out markings on birds or the way they move, and investigate the moon. (See Chapter 10, 'Books'.)

A stop-watch

Stop-clock and stop-watch

Practise using a stop-watch to time events to $\frac{1}{5}$ or $\frac{1}{10}$ s. (Races, passage of cars between two markers along a road, fifty revolutions of a wind vane, etc.)

Compare the accuracy of a stop-watch with that of a stop-clock. With two stop-watches, compare readings of the time for the same event taken by different observers. How much does the result depend on the observer?

Can you use a stop-watch to check the speeds of a record-player?

Schools with science rooms may be able to use a ticker-tape timer (which uses a 6 V or 12 V ac supply from a transformer). Every $\frac{1}{50}$ s a dot is made on a tape as it moves through the instrument. If the tape is fixed to a stone, the time taken for it to fall from a table to the floor can be measured.

See also 'Inventing timers' in *Structures and forces Stage 3*, 'Measuring reaction times' in *Time* and *Ourselves*.

An interest in clocks, the history of time measurement, or astronomy might develop for some children.

Thermometers

The most useful are those measuring from 0 to 110°C and clinical thermometers are interesting.

How do you use clinical thermometers? How long do you have to leave them under someone's tongue before they stop going up? Why don't they go down again? What happens when you shake them?

Using clinical thermometers, can you find if everyone in a class has the same temperature? (Be particular about cleanliness, washing the thermometers in disinfectant solution between each test.)

How much hotter are you after running for 2 minutes?

It is worth letting children spend quite a long time measuring temperatures in many different places for practice; in the middle of the room, over a radiator, near the window, near the bottom of the door, near the ceiling, in a refrigerator, under the cold tap, under the hot tap and so on. You will need a thermometer going to a higher temperature to test ovens.

Expanded polystyrene feels warm. Use a thermometer to find out whether it really is warmer than the room.

Use thermometers for regular measurements of outside temperatures for weather records.

How long does it take an aspirin tablet to dissolve in the same volume of water at different temperatures? You could do the same tests with equal amounts of salt or of sugar.

What is the temperature of melting ice? What happens if you sprinkle a little salt on the ice? Do other substances have the same effect as the salt?

Light-meters

Children are often familiar with the use of these for taking photographs. One may often be borrowed.

How bright is it in different parts of the room, out in the playground, in a wood, coming out of a wood (ie near the edge), in an open field? Compare plants growing in different amounts of shade. Are the species different? Does any one species grow differently?

Use a light-meter to compare the amount of light reflected by different surfaces (eg walls, a mirror, dark and light clothes).

Compare the amount of light transmitted by different numbers of polythene bags, different numbers of sheets of paper.

Compare the amount of light transmitted by an aquarium tank full of clean tap water and the same tank full of water from a polluted river.

It is hoped that in some of their work children will be able to use a camera for recording and for this they should be encouraged to use a light-meter in order to judge the correct exposure.

pH paper (Universal test paper)

This is a paper which is soaked in a dye which changes colour according to how acid a condition it is in. It is sold in strips with a colour code to go with it. Don't let the mysterious letters pH worry anyone at this stage. Simply remember that pH1 is very acid and the paper is red. As conditions get less and less acid, the paper will change through orange and yellow to a greenish yellow and the pH numbers up to pH7. This is *neutral,* not acid at all. From pH7 to pH14 things become more and more *alkaline.* This is the opposite of acid. The pH paper only works for liquids and solutions. You can damp powders and soil with water and press the paper on to them. (Clean hands are very important or you measure the acidity of what you touched last with your fingers!)

Use the paper to test various household liquids, eg vinegar, cooking oil, washing-up liquid, wine, beer, Coca-Cola, lemonade.

Test saliva, milk, fruits (lemon, pear, apple, grape, grapefruit).

Test Alka-Seltzer solution, Milk of Magnesia, etc.

Test soil from different gardens and different places such as woodland, a pasture field, a marshy place, a roadside verge. Dig a hole and test soil from different depths. Perhaps a better way than simply damping the soil and pressing on the paper is to shake up a little of the soil in a clean tube with water, let the solid matter settle and then dip the test paper in the liquid.

Try making your own indicator dyes. Use beetroot, elderberries, red cabbage, petals from flowers (particularly bright red and bright blue ones like geraniums and delphiniums—but try them all). These materials are mashed up, boiled with water and then the coloured liquid is strained off and allowed to evaporate until the colour is fairly strong. The liquid itself can be used to do the tests with or it can be soaked into strips of white blotting paper. Of course you have to test it against a standard paper first to see at what point on the scale colour changes do take place.

Hygrometer

We often need to measure dampness more accurately than our skins can sense it. For example, we may be comparing the plants and animals which live in different conditions or finding the humidity of the atmosphere for weather records or for keeping the conditions right in a textile mill.

A way of using cobalt chloride paper to test dampness is described in the Unit *Trees*.

A much more usable instrument is a direct-reading, 'paper' hygrometer like the one shown. (See Chapter 10.)

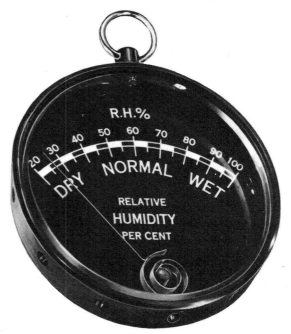

It is interesting to make a model paper hygrometer to see how it works.

Try the model out in a warm, dry living room and in a moisture-laden bathroom or greenhouse.

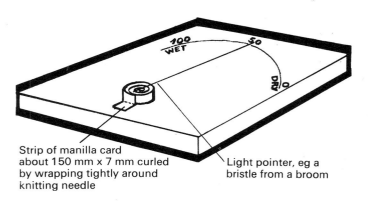

Strip of manilla card about 150 mm x 7 mm curled by wrapping tightly around knitting needle

Light pointer, eg a bristle from a broom

Some schools will have a wet and dry bulb thermometer to measure humidity for weather records. It is difficult to understand at this stage though perfectly easy to read mechanically.

Ammeters and voltmeters

In the experiments on pages 14–15 it was found that the brightness of a bulb was not a very good way of assessing the amount of current flowing.

Children at Stage 3 could use a robust ammeter, 0–1 A, 0–5 A, in circuits such as that shown on page 30 and also a voltmeter, 0–5 V, 0–15 V. (Standard 'Nuffield' equipment—see Chapter 10.)

The ammeter measures the current flowing in amps.

The voltmeter measures the 'pressure' of electricity across any two points in volts. (In this case the battery terminals.)

An ammeter must *never* be connected directly across a battery. Teachers should always check circuits before batteries are actually connected.

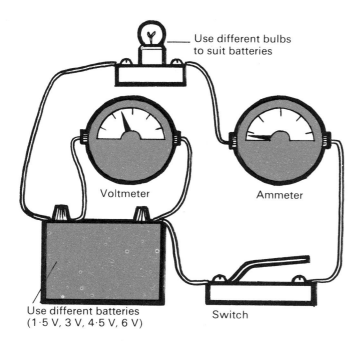

Use different bulbs to suit batteries

Voltmeter

Ammeter

Use different batteries (1·5 V, 3 V, 4·5 V, 6 V)

Switch

Does the voltmeter read the same if connected across the screws of the bulb-holder?

Use different batteries (1·5 V, 3 V, 4·5 V, 6 V) and the bulbs to suit them. Make lists of readings. What happens to the results when the batteries are running down?

Try 6 V and 3·5 V bulbs with 4·5 V, 3 V and 1·5 V batteries. Try a 2·5 V bulb with 3 V and 1·5 V batteries.

Markings on bulbs are often not very clear. It is helpful to paint a colour code on the bulbs and to keep them in boxes marked with the voltage in the same colour. Bulbs rated at 3·5 V can be used on 4·5 V batteries and 2·5 V bulbs on 3 V batteries, but do not overload any others, and take special care to use 1·5 V bulbs only on 1·5 V batteries.

In place of the bulb put various wire-wound resistors (see Chapter 10) of from 5 Ω to 50 Ω.

More can be found out about something which may have been tried before (see page 14).

In the circuit shown, what happens if the distance apart of the plates is varied? (*Don't let them touch.*)

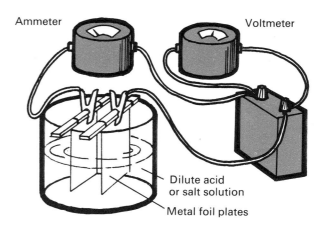

Ammeter

Voltmeter

Dilute acid or salt solution

Metal foil plates

If you double the distance apart, do you halve the current?

Does the area of the plates under water matter?

If you double the area do you double the current?

What happens with *two* batteries in series?

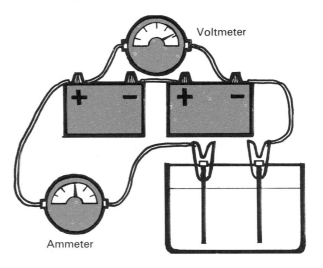

Voltmeter

Ammeter

Which range of the voltmeter will it be necessary to use?

What happens with two batteries wired in parallel?

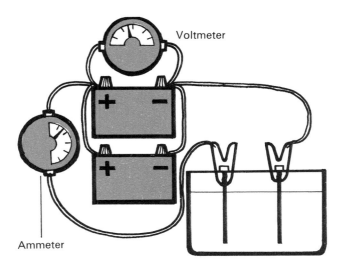

Voltmeter

Ammeter

Inventing measurers

Instead of simply using manufactured instruments it is often a good challenge to make measurers and testers for ourselves. These could be to test hardness, strength, porosity, 'bendability', etc. Some detailed help will be found in the Units *Working with wood Stages 1 and 2; Metals Stages 1 and 2; Children and plastics Stages 1 and 2* and *Structures and forces Stages 1 and 2* and *Stage 3.*

5 Sorting out

Different sets of things

Some things have similar properties, others are entirely different.

Make up sets of things which have something in common:

Red things, woollen things, pictures of eyes (noses, ears), bricks, smooth stones, powders, leaves, electric light bulbs, batteries, cans, boxes, bottles, stamps.

There are very many possibilities and it is fun for everyone to produce a different interesting set.

Look out for the possibility of sub-sets. For example a set labelled 'Food' could be divided in several ways, animal source, vegetable source; home produced, foreign; carbohydrate, protein, etc.

Collect pieces of all the kinds of cloth you can find. Sort them out into cloths made from cotton, from wool, from flax, from silk, from man-made fibres, from mixtures.

Are there any others? What about mohair, alpaca and hessian?

How many *names* of cotton cloths can you find?

How many names of woollen cloths, man-made fibre cloths, etc, can you collect? Use lenses and microscopes to find what the differences are, if you can.

There is no need to spend a long time on the above.

Once the idea that making a set involves looking for a chosen common property, mixtures of things may be collected to be sorted into two or three sets. Some examples might be:

Small pebbles and sand; wood, metal and plastics objects; red, green and yellow objects; rough and smooth things; things with rounded edges and sharp edges; crystals and powders; transparent, translucent and opaque objects; screws with different type heads; rigid and flexible things; objects which float and those which sink.

Each child should try to make up a 'mixture' to try out on the others.

In some cases there will be more than one way of sorting out, for example the screws may not only divide into sets with countersunk heads, half-round heads or Phillips heads, but also into japanned, brass, steel and plated finishes or into different sizes.

Encourage children to look for different ways of classifying.

Odd man out

Next, pick the odd man out in sets of things. Some examples might be:

Mixed coloured objects with only one yellow one.

Nails with only one oval one.

Coins of the same denomination but one of slightly different design (at the moment we are restricted to

5p and 10p values).

A collection of similar objects such as cotton reels, one of which has been made a little heavier without any visible signs. In this case all the holes in the reels may be closed up at the ends but one reel will have lead or sand packed in the hole first.

An exactly similar set of reels could be made with only one *not* weighted.

Pieces of card, hardboard, etc, in squares of many sizes with one piece not quite square.

A similar set of circles with one slightly out of true.

A set of balls, one filed slightly flat so that it doesn't roll well (polystyrene balls or ball-bearings).

A set of similar objects with one 'doctored' invisibly to give an odd position for the centre of gravity.

A set of objects only one of which is magnetic.

A set of objects only one of which conducts electricity (the carbon rod from a battery is difficult to spot as a conductor).

A set of insects (alive or mounted) and one centipede.

A set of non-flowering plants (mosses, ferns, lichens, fungi) and one specimen of pearlwort (which grows on most lawns and is called a moss but is not).

A set of grasses and one rush or sedge.

It will be found that the discovery of the odd man out may involve considerable skill. Often it can be done in more than one way and as long as the choice can be justified it is, of course, correct.

Children are usually very keen to make up their own puzzle for others to do. One child brought a card on which were Sellotaped many strands of coloured wool but it took even the girls some time to work out that all were 3-ply except one which was 2-ply.

Needless to say this work is very good for creating good discussions.

The chromosomes of a human female (left) and a human male (right) showing the twenty-two pairs of autosomes and the one pair of sex chromosomes. How do the male and female chromosomes differ?

Small differences

Some things are as different as chalk and cheese. (These traditional opposites are not so different visually—break a wedge of chalk and put it amongst some pieces of lighter-coloured cheeses.)

But small differences are interesting. One could collect together a set of cheeses. What are *all* the differences? It will be found that all the senses except hearing are involved.

Perhaps it would be well to work on a simpler one. How many different *bottles* can we collect? There are differences in material, size, shape, weight, colour, contents, labels, marks in the material, kind of stopper, length of neck, country of origin.

Or could we look at *feet*? How many differences are there in feet? One could collect animal pictures, go to a zoo, look at pets, look at small animals outside, take our shoes off. The whole set 'feet' is rather large but even if we keep to one species—ourselves—there will be many differences all over the world.

Suppose we look at the feet of children in our class.

There will still be differences. How many can you find? How many children have their second toe longer than their big toe? How many shorter?

What about hair, eyes, ears, hands, teeth? (See the Unit *Ourselves*.)

On the right are some different children's eyes.

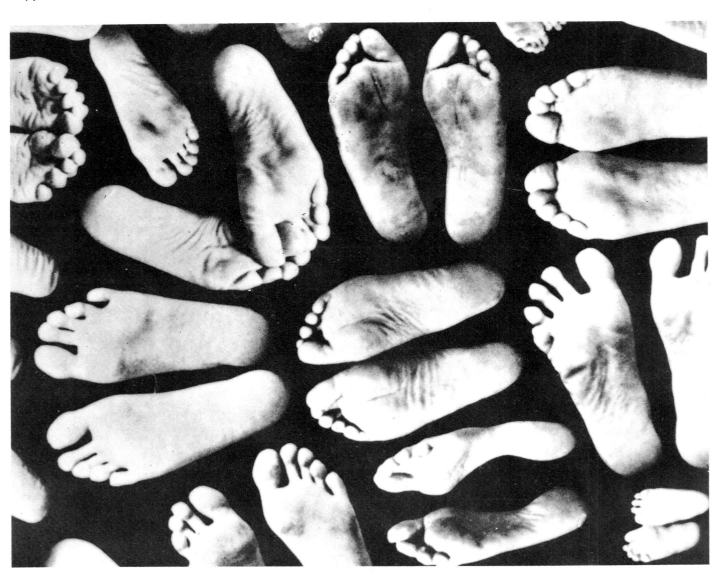

Here are some further ideas for making sets of similar things with interesting differences.

Boxes, cans.
Spoons, knives, forks, tea-pots, etc.
Breeds of dogs, rabbits or other pets.
Kinds of flour, sugar, washing powders.
Kinds of paper, cloth, soil, nails.

How many different kinds of doors can you find?

One group found fifty-four kinds of nails. They were made of iron, galvanised iron, copper and brass and included even a steeplejack's nail and some clog nails.

What is the history of the nail?

Why are tacks always a blue colour?

A plastics tissue is now manufactured for wrapping meat and fish and for making food bags.

How many tests can you devise to show that it is not paper?

How fine do you want to go?

We could go on looking closer and closer. We could take the finger prints of everyone in the class and then we should *all* be different.

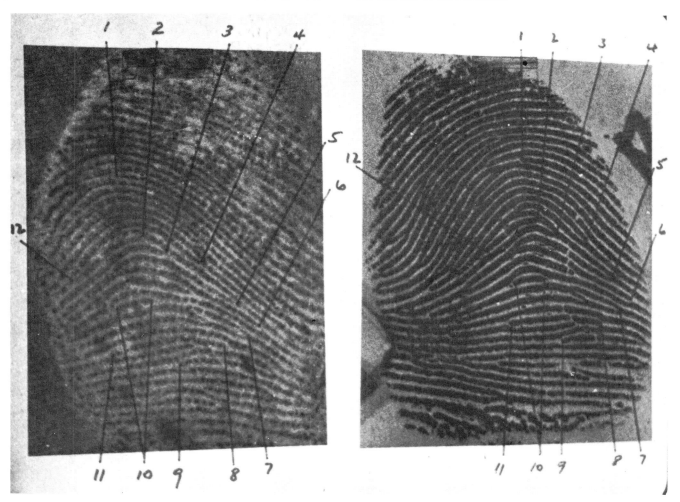

The print from the scene of the crime (left) matches one in police records (right) at all the numbered points

With our set of bottles we could use hand-lenses and look for scratches. We could record exactly where the spots were on our dogs and rabbits.

When we classify things we must decide how fine is the detail we intend to look at.

Here are some interesting fine details to look for:

Earwigs

Collect earwigs in specimen tubes. This is easy in summer and autumn as you can shake them out of flower petals (especially dahlias). With a lens or a ×20 microscope count the segments on their antennae. Make sets each having different numbers of segments and draw a column graph showing how many earwigs in each set.

The more segments, the older the earwig.

Woodlice

Woodlice are easy to find under stones, old bits of wood and rotting organic material in damp places. Collect some in damp jars. Can you see any different kinds? There may be a small pink one, often found on rockeries, but the others may seem rather alike. Look at

their antennae and rear ends with a good lens. You may spot the difference between the species shown in the drawing.

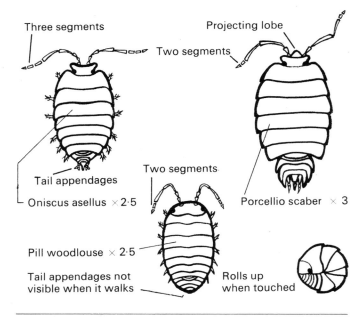

Three segments
Two segments
Tail appendages
Oniscus asellus × 2·5

Projecting lobe
Two segments
Porcellio scaber × 3

Two segments
Pill woodlouse × 2·5
Tail appendages not visible when it walks
Rolls up when touched

Variation

Small differences in one species of living things are called variations. We have seen some already. Human beings have variations in the shape of their feet, colour of their skin, hair, eyes and so on.

Measure the heights of everyone in your school of one age within a month (eg all the nine-year-olds whose birthdays are in May).

Who is the shortest? Who is the tallest? What is the variation? Are several children the same height? Draw a graph showing the number of children of each height. If you draw a separate graph for boys and girls are they different?

Try ten-year-olds, eleven-year-olds, twelve-year-olds.

Try weights instead of heights.

If you can collect figures for a greater number of children than those in one school does the shape of the graph change?

From an area of turf where there are patches of clover collect clover leaves with different patterns. How many variations can you find? One group working on a demolition site in a northern city found fifty-seven.

Five of the many variations of the pattern on clover leaves

How many leaf patterns can you find in zonal geraniums?

How many different designs can you find on pansy flowers?

Collect land snails of one species. (Banded snails are good for this experiment.) How many variations of pattern can you find on their shells?

41

How many variations of ivy leaves can you find? Look for variations in size, shape and colour. Are the variations related to the position on the tree in which the leaf is growing, the amount of sun or shade, which particular tree or bush is inspected?

Do a similar study for holly, maple or hawthorn leaves.

How much variation can you find in dandelion leaves or the leaves of the hoary plantain (*Plantago media*)?

Take the seeds from one packet and grow the plants in identical conditions. All the seeds must have the same soil (preferably sterilised seed compost), the same temperature, light and air. What variations do you get in say 100 plants? Do some species of plants show more variations than others? Most likely the seeds in the packet came from several plants. See what variation you get with seeds you collect yourself from the *one* plant.

If we wonder how closely to look for differences, the answer is that we should simply suit our needs.

If we just want to sort chalk from cheese there is no need to know the difference between Gorgonzola and Cheddar, but if you are a grocer or a gourmet there is.

An astronomer may at one time be measuring distances in the universe in *light years* (the distance light travels in a year, at a speed of 300 million metres per second) and at another the wavelength of light from a star in millionths of a metre.

Detectives deal in the pattern of fingerprints, dentists in the pattern of the fillings in their patients' teeth.

Many scientific activities require the consideration of very small differences, in the arrangements of atoms perhaps, or even of the parts inside an atom. We may say 'As like as two peas in a pod', yet two peas from one pod might grow into two very different plants; one might be tall with yellow seeds and the other dwarf with green seeds. To see the difference in the two peas before we planted them we should need some way of seeing the arrangement of the genes in the cells.

6 Differences which form a sequence

Sequence sets

The objects in a set are sometimes related to one another in the sense that they make up a sequence or series when arranged in the right order. Here are some examples:

Russian dolls, nests of tables, grades of petrol, jars, cans or boxes of products sold in different sizes.

Sets of screwdrivers, spanners, feeler gauges and other tools (and of course, the screws, nuts, etc, that the tools fit).

Metal, timber, card, plastics sheet sold in different thicknesses.

Wire sold in different diameters.

Music
In musical instruments we have very well-known sets of notes.

What instruments have sets of different-sized bars to hit?

In which other instruments do you make a note by hitting something? How does the note vary as you change the size of the thing that is hit?

Which instruments have sets of strings? What different arrangements are there? What different materials and dimensions for the strings?

How do you get a different note from one string?

What difference does the length of string make to the note?

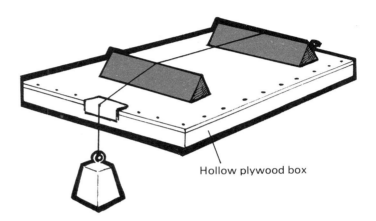

Hollow plywood box

What difference does the tension in the string make?

What difference do the material and the diameter of the string make? Try thick and thin parcel string, thick and thin wires of different metals, violin strings, guitar strings and so on.

How do you get different notes from a piano?

An orchestra has instruments in related sets. Can you name the string set, the woodwind set and the brass set?

Sound is made when things vibrate fairly fast. To our ears certain numbers of vibrations per second (Hertz) sound pleasant. Pleasant sounds seem to be made by vibrations whose speed is related. Try sounding middle C on a piano. The string vibrates 256 times a second (256 Hertz).

There is a note higher up which sounds similar. The vibrations to make this are 512 Hertz, just twice as many.

Note	C	D	E	F	G	A	B	C	D	E	F	G	A	B	C
Hertz	128	144	160	170	192	213	240	256	288	320	341	384	427	480	512

Similarly the next note lower down which sounds similar is made by strings vibrating at 128 Hertz.

Between these notes we can find six which seem to 'mix in' very pleasantly. The table above shows the number of vibrations per second to make them.

From one C to the next, the ratios of these vibrations are:

C	D	E	F	G	A	B	C
1	$\frac{9}{8}$	$\frac{5}{4}$	$\frac{4}{3}$	$\frac{3}{2}$	$\frac{5}{3}$	$\frac{15}{8}$	2

In music then, the pleasant sounds seem to repeat themselves in eights and a set of eight notes is called an *octave.*

Find the difference in size and weight of two tuning forks for notes an octave apart. Do the same for chime bars or the notes of a xylophone.

Can you make a xylophone from pieces of wood? How do the sizes have to be related?

Compare the qualities of the notes from oak, deal and other kinds of woods.

Look at many musical instruments and find what changes have to be made in order to play two notes an octave apart.

Look at musical instruments from other countries where they might find a different sequence of vibrations pleasant to the ear.

Glue on felt, sponge rubber or expanded polystyrene

A sitar from India

Chemistry (a background note)

The idea of octaves fascinated an English chemist called Newlands. In 1866, he arranged the chemical elements in order of their atomic weight and pointed out that if they were divided into groups like this:

Li	Be	B	C	N	O	F
Na	Mg	Al	Si	P	S	Cl
K	Ca	Sc	Ti	V	Cr	Mn

There was a 'kind of repetition' in their properties; the elements in each column behaved in a similar way. He called this the Law of Octaves.

Most people laughed at the idea although there did seem to be a similarity between the elements in the columns. Unfortunately if you took *all* the known elements the idea didn't fit. This was partly because some elements had then not been discovered and the gaps that Newlands could not allow for, quite spoiled his 'harmony'.

However, the idea started chemists looking for a sequence and trying to put all the elements into some sort of a related set. The man who really managed to do it was the Russian, Mendeleev. He made the first satisfactory Periodic Table of Elements.

The atoms from which the whole universe is composed are found to be related to each other in quite remarkable sequences.

Some other series of things to investigate

Animals' legs

Can you find names of animals with different numbers of legs? Arrange in lists of 0, 2, 4, 6, 8, 10, 12, 14 and more than 30 (one centipede from Central America has more than 700).

Why are there no odd numbers?

Mollusc shells

Collect mollusc shells. They could be from the seashore, from fresh water or from snails which live on land. How many kinds can you find? Sort into shells with one part and shells with two parts (bivalves like cockles, muscles, oysters, razor shells, tellina). Take care here. When the animal is dead the two parts of the bivalve shells come apart, but you can always tell which was the inside surface. The spiral shells can be sorted into those like a spire and the 'flat' spiral ones like a coil of rope.

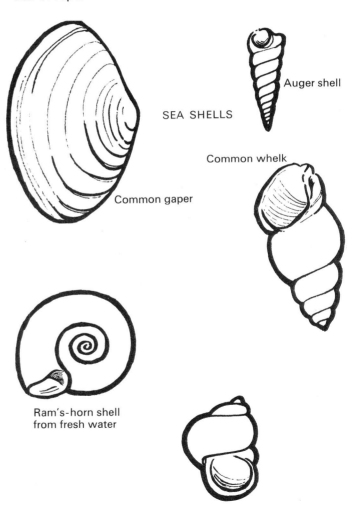

SEA SHELLS

Auger shell

Common whelk

Common gaper

Ram's-horn shell from fresh water

Shell of garden snail

If you hold the opening of the spire type facing you with the point at the top, you may find you have some shells which wind round to the left and some which wind round to the right.

These shells, and the creatures inside them, grow in size but do not change shape. The shell grows at the end or edge only.

Draw a straight line across some of these shells from the 'starting point' to the edge. Measure the width of the whorls or the distances between rings to see how they have grown.

Keep fresh-water snails in an aquarium. They will lay eggs in a blob of jelly which you will find stuck to the sides or to some water-weed. Watch the young snails developing. When they hatch, look at them with a hand lens or better still in a little water under a ×20 microscope.

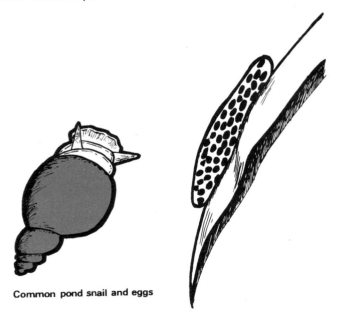

Common pond snail and eggs

Compare the shell they are born with, with that of a grown snail.

Which bit of the adult snail's shell did it start life with?

Other spirals

What other spirals can you find? Some examples would be:

Coiled ropes, springs, orb-webs of spiders, electric lamp filaments, the elements of electric fires, some staircases, the centre part of toilet rolls, tendrils of peas or clematis, the climbing stems of bindweed or runner-beans, the floret arrangement of a sunflower, screws and bolts, telephone cords, the metal flexible tubes of showers.

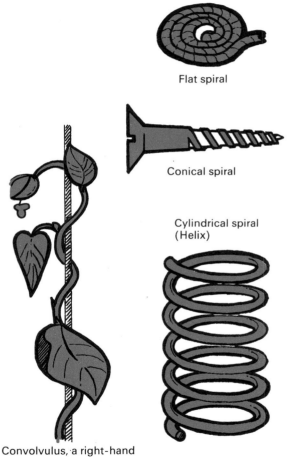

Flat spiral

Conical spiral

Cylindrical spiral (Helix)

Convolvulus, a right-hand (clockwise) spiral

Sort them into left-handed and right-handed spirals and into flat, cylindrical and conical spirals.

Drawing spirals

1. An easy method for drawing spirals is shown in the illustration:

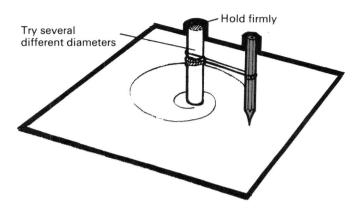

Try several different diameters

Hold firmly

Sellotape one end of a piece of string to a cylindrical object. This may be a piece of broomstick or other rod, a piece of rigid tubing or a cylindrical jar or can. Wrap the string round a few times and Sellotape the other end to a pencil or felt pen. Hold the cylinder firmly on a large sheet of paper and, keeping the string taut, draw the spiral as you unwind it. Two people will probably be needed unless the central cylinder can be fixed by a clamp.

2. Start with a point O in the middle of a piece of paper. Draw radiating lines at 10-degree intervals.

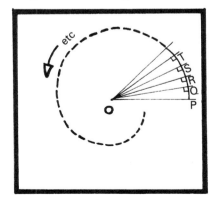

Starting at P draw the line PQ so that angle OQP is a right angle (a set-square is useful). Continue with

QR, etc, in the same way making several complete turns and finishing off with a good freehand curve.

3. Another kind of spiral can be drawn first by drawing a circle. Next cut out a cardboard right-angle like a carpenter's try-square with the short arm equal to the radius of the circle. The other arm should be more than three times as long.

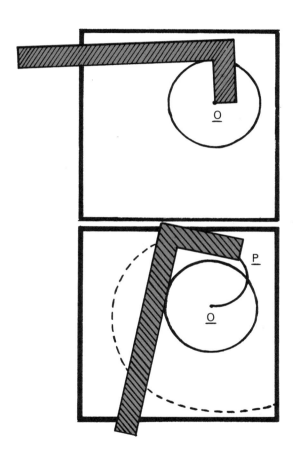

The long arm is rolled around the circle, just touching it all the time, while the corner P is marked on the paper.

Try various sizes for the circle you start with (not too big unless you are working on a very large sheet of paper).

Arrangement of leaves on stems

Look at the position of leaves on stems of shrubs and other plants. Try privet and rhododendron for example.

Start with one leaf on a stem and then look for the next one higher up in an exactly similar position. Count the number of leaves and the number of turns round the stem to come to this position.

It is a help to tie a thread to the bottom leaf and wind it round as shown. In the picture, three leaves may be counted in one turn round the stem.

Write down all the cases you can find:

Number of turns	0	1	1	2	3	5
Number of leaves	1	2	3	5	8	13

Do you notice any connection between the figures? (Pick any one and add the two previous ones together—this is called a Fibbonachi series.)

The result of leaves being arranged in this way seems to be that each receives a maximum amount of sunlight.

Graphs show relationships

Graphs are useful for showing whether sets of measurements are related. One school near the Severn estuary was interested in the tide tables. The numbers seemed to be related somehow. They tried plotting graphs of the times of high tide at a certain place each day.

You might like to collect woodlice (see page 40) and make a graph of their sizes as one group did. On the last day of April they collected 322 and measured them in millimetres. Children find it quite easy to hold them gently and do this. They were placed in damp dishes in groups.

Size	Number
mm	
5 or less	33
6– 7	28
8– 9	26
10–11	62
12–13	102
14–15	55
16–17	15
18–19	1
20 and over	0

A very interesting thing was that a group working at the same job seven weeks before produced a different graph.

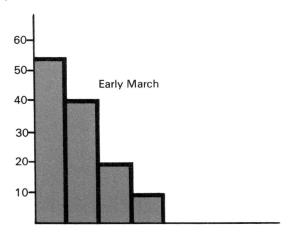

Early March

Can you explain the change?

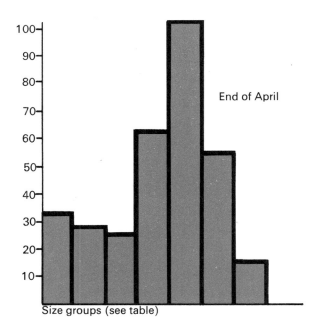

End of April

Size groups (see table)

A graph was drawn and the animals carefully returned to their habitat without harm.

7 Separating things

It is very important for us to be able to separate things out. Sorting sheep from goats is easy. The next step, sorting *your* sheep from *my* sheep or one-year-olds from two-year-olds, involves more detailed observation and the invention of a system of marking.

In the sophisticated life of the twentieth century we have reached the stage where our transport, our heating, our power supply and even our health depend on the separation of the large number of fractions contained in crude oil or in coal.

Ways of separating things

By hand and eye
Try sorting out money by hand as a bank clerk does.

Can you invent a coin-sorting apparatus?

Is it quicker than using your hands?

Is it as accurate?

What are the differences between large, medium and small eggs?

How big are the differences?

Can you sort out a mixed lot of eggs by hand?

Could you make some simple apparatus to help?

Would it work on weight or linear measurement?

Is one way more accurate than another?

Some products have to be sorted by other criteria than size, shape and weight, for example by colour or by whether they are fresh or have gone bad. It is said that you can sort good peas from bad peas for canning by the way they bounce. Can you find out if this is true? Try this test before cooking and after cooking the peas.

Have a mixture of objects made from all kinds of material.

Pick out the iron things by hand.

How could you do it more quickly?

Sort out iron filings from a mixture with copper, aluminium (or other metallic filings or turnings), sand, sulphur, etc.

Sieves
Can you make a home-made sieve from a metal foil plate or dish to separate sand and small pebbles from a mixture?

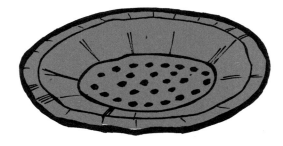

Can you make a *set* of sieves to sort out lentils, peas and beans?

How do you work out what size to make the holes? (See *Holes, gaps and cavities* for more things to do.)

One flour manufacturer would have us imagine in his advertisement that they employ little bowler-hatted men for 'grading grains'. Actually they do it with a very large and complicated system of shaking sieves.

Can you find out anything about the size of flour grains with your microscope? Do they vary very much? You will have to spread a very small amount of flour out very thinly preferably on black paper.

How do the flour grains compare with other powders, say plaster of Paris or bicarbonate of soda?

How do pollen grains from different flowers vary?

Use a set of sieves (see Chapter 10) for sorting out the particle sizes in different samples of soils. Soil may be collected from perhaps a wood, a moor, a roadside, a 'clayey' place, a sandy place, the side of a stream, etc. (If there is vegetation, the top few centimetres of soil are removed before collecting the sample.) Dry the sample thoroughly, break up any lumps and pick out any obviously large stones or bits of debris. Use the same weight, say 100 g, for each test.

Shake the soil well through each size of sieve, starting with the largest mesh. Weigh (to 1 g) what is left on each sieve and what goes through the finest sieve.

Make column graphs.

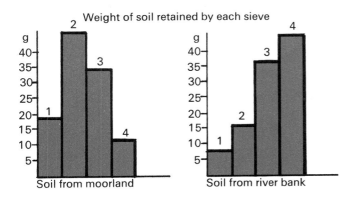

Weight of soil retained by each sieve

Soil from moorland

Soil from river bank

How do the soils you have collected differ in particle sizes?

Settling

An easier way of sorting out the particle sizes of different soils is to shake them with water.

Put about 3 cm of each sample in a tube with a flat base and a stopper.

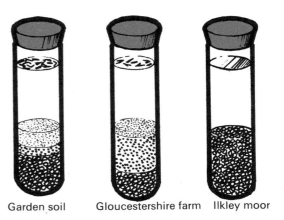

Garden soil   Gloucestershire farm   Ilkley moor

These are easily obtained as many supermarkets sell such things as cake decorations in them, but they are cheap to buy as specimen tubes (see Chapter 10). A good size is 100 mm high by 25 mm diameter, and plastic, even though it soon scratches, is preferable to glass.

Three-quarters fill the tubes with water, put on the stopper and shake well for at least a minute. *Immediately* you stop shaking put the tube on a level surface and allow to settle for several hours. Measure any layers you can see.

How have the particles arranged themselves?

Why do the large ones sink first? Don't heavy weights fall at the same speed as light ones?

Does anything float in any of the tubes? If it does, what do you think it might be?

Use your lens and microscope to find out if you are right.

Panning for gold

In the gold-rush days, prospectors found that there was quite a lot of the metal in the alluvium of the bed of streams. It was mostly in small 'specks' and they got it out by 'panning'.

How good are you at panning for gold?

I don't suppose you will have much luck in the local river bed but you could make up some test material to try out the technique. Real gold is likely to be too expensive for most schools too, but you could take a few very small pieces of lead (perhaps trimmed from **bits** of roof flashing) and coat them with gold paint. (This is a reasonably fair substitute; gold is nearly **twice** as heavy as lead and so would separate even better.)

Next you will need an old large frying pan without a handle or a similar shallow circular dish with sloping sides.

Work outside where it doesn't matter if you make a mess.

Count out a number of your 'gold' bits and mix them very well with enough sand, gravel and soil to fill the pan about three-quarters full.

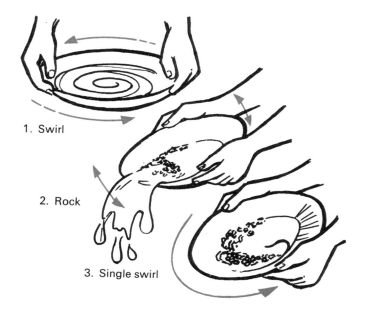

1. Swirl

2. Rock

3. Single swirl

Fill the dish to the brim with water and swirl round and round to get clay and mud suspended in the water.

Pour off, fill up with clean water and repeat several times.

There may also be some lumps to break up and stones you could pick out.

When the water remains fairly clean change to rocking the pan backwards and forwards allowing the water and any materials which rise with it to spill over the front of the pan.

After repeating this several times you will have left just heavy material on the bottom. Give this a single swirl and pick out any 'gold'. Repeat the swirl and see if you can pick any more.

Did you get *all* your bits of gold out?

Decanting and filtering

In the home we often need to separate solids from liquids. First of all we can pour off as much liquid as possible without stirring up the solid. This is called *decanting.* Try decanting some liquids with a sediment in them like vinegar or wine. Pouring tea off the leaves and coffee off the grounds is really decanting.

A better job is made by *filtering.* In the kitchen we usually use sieves as filters, for example when we pour out coffee and tea, or separate boiled rice from the water it is boiled in.

Have you ever made crab-apple jelly?

Wash the apples, weigh them and chop them up (skins, cores and all!) and cover with water.

Boil until everything is soft and mushy.

Then filter off the liquid. (Clean muslin makes a good filter.)

The lovely pink liquid is now boiled with sugar, 1 lb of sugar to every pint ($\frac{1}{2}$ kg to $\frac{1}{2}$ l), until a little of the syrup sets when placed on a saucer in a cool place for a time.

With much work in chemistry, the solid we want to separate is precipitated and usually is much too fine to separate with any ordinary sieve. Then filter paper is used, the holes in this being very fine.

The drawing shows one way of folding a circular filter paper to go into a filter funnel.

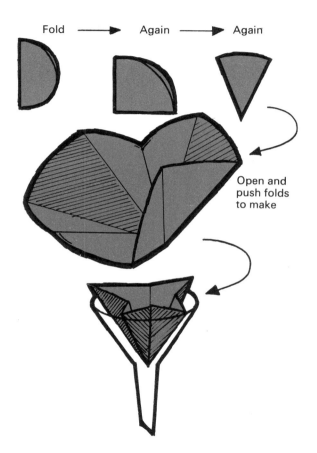

Fold ⟶ Again ⟶ Again

Open and push folds to make

Dissolve some Epsom salts and some washing soda in hot water in separate containers. Then mix together.

What happens?

Can you filter off the solid?

Find out how our water supply is filtered.

Make a model water filter in a plant-pot and test whether it works with slightly muddy water.

Will it take the salt out of salty water?

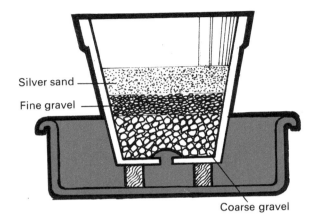

Silver sand

Fine gravel

Coarse gravel

Separating liquids from liquids

This is fairly easy if the liquids don't mix. Let them settle in a transparent jug and then pour off the top one. This is decanting again. The drawing shows a separating funnel which is useful for drawing off the *bottom* liquid.

But what can you do if one liquid mixes with (dissolves in) the other, like methylated spirit and water? (See page 55).

Evaporating

How can you get the salt out of sea water? Can you filter it out?

Evaporating brine

The picture shows what is done in hot countries.

Could we boil off the water to get the salt?

The picture shows the laboratory way of doing it.

There is no reason why you should not use an old pan on a stove. In either case it must be carefully watched

as it comes towards dryness and the heat then turned down very much.

If you don't live near the sea you will have to make up the 'sea water'.

Try retrieving other solids from solution in water, eg Epsom salts, washing soda, alum. Sugar will give a surprising result.

Is there anything dissolved in tap water? How can you find out?

Crystallising

What happens if you let evaporation take place *slowly*?

Make saturated solutions of salt, sugar and alum, ie stir as much solid into water as will dissolve. Take the clear solution (how are you going to get it away from the excess solid?), put it in a clean dish in a cupboard or other place away from dust and let it stand. Be patient, don't disturb the dish for a long time.

What happens?

What *shape* are the crystals? (To answer this, use a lens or the ×20 microscope.)

There will be many clumps of crystals and imperfect ones; sort out the perfect ones.

You may be able to try copper sulphate, ammonium nitrate, magnesium sulphate (Epsom salts) and sodium thiosulphate (hypo) as well.

Collect specimens of rocks and look for crystals with your lens. Break pieces with a hammer and look again. How could these crystals have got there?

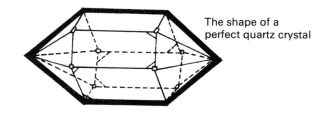

The shape of a perfect quartz crystal

Rock crystals

Distilling

If we had wanted to get pure water out of sea water instead of the salt, or if we had wanted to separate two liquids, we should have used *distillation*. Different liquids have different boiling points and so, if a mixture is heated, each liquid boils off at a different temperature. The vapour may be cooled back to a liquid and the different 'fractions' collected.

Try distilling ink or slightly muddy water in the apparatus shown.

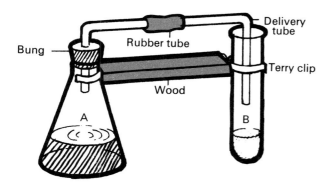

(This is described fully in Nuffield Combined Science *Teachers' Guide I*, page 95; *Teacher's Guide II*, page 198 and *Teachers' Guide III*, page 17.)

The ink or muddy water is heated in the conical flask *A* until it boils. The steam boiling off is condensed to clean water in the tube *B*.

Parts to order for the apparatus are given in Chapter 10.

Centrifuging

If some oils are shaken up vigorously with water they form an *emulsion*. They break up into small drops which stay dispersed and do not settle out, at least not for a long time. Cod-liver oil, olive oil, and cooking oils will do this.

If solid particles are fine enough they also will stay suspended in a liquid. An example is the red blood corpuscles suspended in blood plasma.

Fog is a suspension of very fine water particles in air.

The parts of an emulsion may be separated by spinning in a centrifuge. A model could be made as shown.

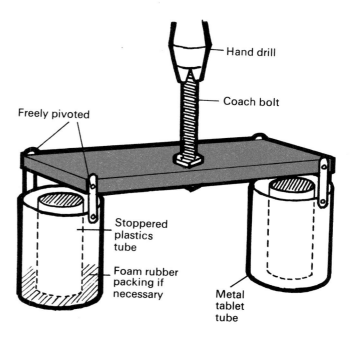

For safety, the model should be protected with a large pan when in use. The drill is pushed through a hole in a board which rests on the pan and has blocks to hold it in the right position.

The model is inefficient and little more than a demonstration of how a centrifuge works. Perhaps some teachers will be able to demonstrate an electrically driven one in a laboratory.

Chromatography
Simple experiments in separating colours are described in *Structures and forces Stage 3* and in *Change Stages 1 and 2*. This method is the only simple way of separating some closely similar chemicals such as the amino-acids.

8 What use is all this?

Dependence on separation methods for the production from raw materials of the things needed for our complicated way of life, has already been mentioned. There follow, briefly, some other uses of sorting out techniques which are worth attention.

Classification

Go to a library. How do you find the science books, the travel books, the novels?

How do you find out if the library has a book by a particular author?

How do you find books on molluscs or microscopes?

Find out how library books are classified.

Whenever there are too many facts to remember easily we sort them out into sets. Look for some of the other uses we make of classification:

Advertisements in newspapers, telephone numbers (two ways), roads, goods in supermarkets, parts in a works or garage store.

Perhaps the best-known classification starts as shown below.

There are other ways of classifying living things. For example it is often done according to the type of place they live in. The whole point about classification is that we do it in the way that best helps our purpose.

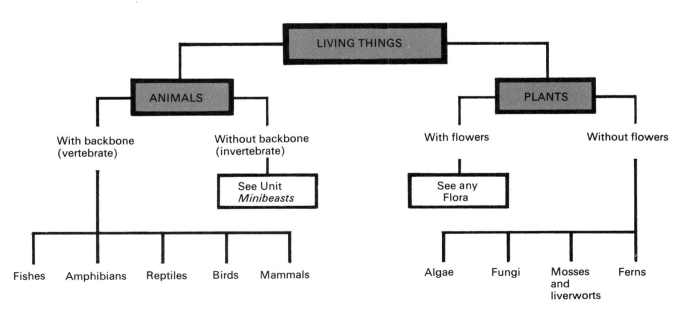

Identifying

Classification helps us to identify readily. Children commonly find great interest in identifying birds, railway engines, aeroplanes, cars, sailing boats, etc, and this could be encouraged.

Often special marks are used to make identification more obvious.

What are the ways of recognising bottles used for poisons?

What are the signs used to mark radio-active materials, flammable liquids, high-voltage wires?

What marks a police car, an ambulance, a fire engine, road-men marking out the white lines, a traffic warden?

What is the colour code used to identify each wire in an electric plug?

Watch cars going along a road for a time. How do you identify the makes, where they were registered and how old they are? Make lists.

How do you identify a wasp? How can you be sure it is not a bee or hoverfly?

Try making some identification *keys*.

The idea behind a 'key' is explained in the Unit *Trees* and you should look at those for slugs and pond animals in *Minibeasts*. Some titles for keys might be:

Flowers on the school field in June.

Birds that come to my garden.

People in our class.

Types of aeroplane

Classes of sailing dinghies.

Remember that good illustrations are vital for good keys.

Children could be given three bottles of colourless liquid to identify (one water, one lime water and one salt water). They are not to assume anything, even that the liquids are non-poisonous (though of course they *must* be). That rules out tasting or trying them on the dog. Quite a puzzle.

Diagnosing

This is a special case of identifying. A doctor diagnoses diseases from symptoms like spots, high temperature or where the pain is. In order to know which kind of influenza is causing an epidemic he has to call in help from specialists with high-powered microscopes in order to recognise a virus.

A garage man diagnoses where the fault is when a car won't go.

Set up simple circuits with a battery, a switch and a bulb. Arrange the circuits to have one of the following faults: broken bulb, run-down battery, broken switch, circuit connected without stripping the insulation from the wire in various places, resistance wire used instead of copper wire.

Who can diagnose the trouble?

As the children become good at it, one can include more than one fault, and even descend to tricks such as putting in a hidden fine wire to short circuit the switch or an almost invisible bit of Sellotape stuck under the springy arm of the switch to prevent it making a conducting contact with the screw.

Some children delight in inventing puzzles like the two shown in the drawing.

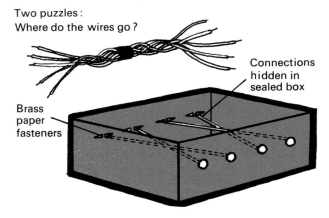

Two puzzles:
Where do the wires go?

Connections hidden in sealed box

Brass paper fasteners

With the bundle of wires, one has to choose a wire at one end and find where it goes to, not forgetting that some wires might end in the middle of the bundle and others bend back and return to the end at which they started.

The puzzle boxes can either be made quite simple with straight-forward connections from a fastener on one side to any one on the other, or more complicated by leaving some fasteners entirely unconnected and having others joined to two or more on the other side.

Choosing

Classification helps us to choose. The yellow pages of the telephone directory illustrate this.

When we can sort out the different kinds of grasses into those that are leafy and those that are stalky, those that various animals prefer, those that make good hay or good silage, those that are tough and will stand a lot of running on, those that regularly grow well whatever the kind of season, those that grow best in damp water-meadows and those which are tough enough for poor soils or bleak hillsides, then we can begin to choose what seeds mixture it is best to sow to feed the cows on a particular farm or to make a football pitch, a cricket pitch or a golf course.

See how many different kinds of grasses you can find (best when they are flowering in June and July).

Grow some grass seed mixtures sold for different purposes and see what differences you can find. Don't finish the experiment as soon as they have sprouted, grow them right on until they flower. This is best done on plots of a square metre outside, though it is possible on trays of compost inside.

When we can classify plants according to the conditions they best like for growing, we can choose the best to suit different soils, aspects, drainage, etc, in farms and gardens.

Can you find out why you don't often see lilacs and rhododendrons growing together?

Nettles seem to grow almost anywhere, but what conditions do they like *best*?

Development of generalisations

When we sort out *observations* and collect them together in groups we may begin to see patterns in these arrangements. We can then often make general rules (laws) which fit the pattern. A great deal of more advanced science is concerned with looking for these general rules.

There follow three very simple examples of generalisations made from observations.

1. A rule about circles
Make a collection of 'circular' things of all sizes:

Rings, discs, cylinders, spheres.

There might be:

Wheels, plates, balls, cans, bottles, coins, pieces of tree trunks, lids (from dustbin size downwards), corks and stoppers.

Measure round them (circumference).

Measure across them (diameter). Make a pair of calipers to do this well.

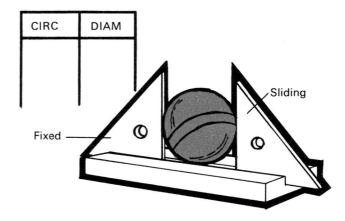

Make a table of all measurements. What do you notice? How could you write down a simple rule?

2. A pattern in growth

Weigh pet mice, hamsters, guinea pigs, kittens, puppies, etc, each day from soon after they are born until they are adult and make graphs.

What do you notice about *all* the growth graphs?

Is there a pattern?

Does it work for human beings?

Collect from families and friends, height and weight records for as large a group as possible of all ages.

Work out averages for each year of age.

Plot one graph for average heights and one for average weights for people of different ages.

Do they fit the pattern?

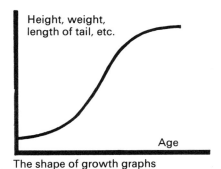

The shape of growth graphs

Next take the figures for children between five and eighteen years old and get *separate* averages for boys and for girls for each year.

Draw graphs for these.

Do you notice anything?

We have been finding some interesting general rules by looking at the shape of graphs.

3. A general rule about reflection

Arrange two blocks of wood near the edge of a table to form a slit. Shine a light from a strong torch through the slit to make a beam and arrange a mirror as shown to reflect the beam.

Work in as dim a place as you can and have the blocks and mirror on a white sheet of paper.

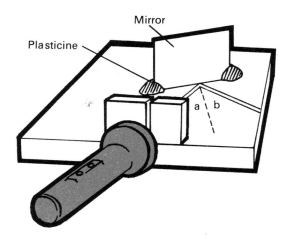

Draw on the paper the lines of the beams of light, the line of the mirror and a line at right angles to the mirror from the point at which the beam is reflected.

What would you guess about angle *a* and angle *b*?

Measure with a folded piece of paper or a protractor to see if your guess is right.

Now change the position of the mirror to try many different angles for the light to strike it.

Is there a general rule?

How could you write it simply?

The great advantage of having spotted a general law or pattern is that it may be used to predict what will happen in unknown situations. For example we may now calculate the angle at which to fix a mirror to see round a corner, or work out how to arrange two mirrors to make a periscope.

Putting things together

A television camera scans a scene, passing over it backwards and forwards 625 times in $\frac{1}{25}$ s and measuring the brightness of the light all the time. The impulses from the camera are broadcast as radio waves but the important thing for us is that we have a set in our homes which will put the separated bits together again to make a picture.

In this Unit we have, for the most part, been sorting, separating and analysing. It is equally important to put together again, to *synthesise*. This is done, not usually to get the same thing back again like the television picture, but—a much more exciting idea—in order to make something *new*.

Here are some examples of this process.

What separate things would you need to get to make concrete, Christmas pudding, fruit cake, a model plane, ginger beer? Where do they come from? How are they put together? What proportions? What treatment is applied?

Make one of these things. How does the resulting product differ from the materials you started with?

How are metals separated out from ores? (See the Unit *Metals Background information.*) Having got metals we can synthesise alloys (eg brass, stainless steel, duralumin). What are some of the things which are made up from metals and their alloys?

What can be synthesised from the separate letters of the alphabet?

An interesting practical activity would be to use chromatography to separate colours and then to put them together again.

A band of, say, black Quink, Boots' edible green or any other water-soluble dye (or even better a mixture) is painted across a strip of blotting paper (or, better, chromatography paper) a short distance from one end,

then the paper is set up as shown.

The rising water washes the colours up the paper at different rates.

When the first colour reaches the top, lift out the paper and cut each colour off with scissors.

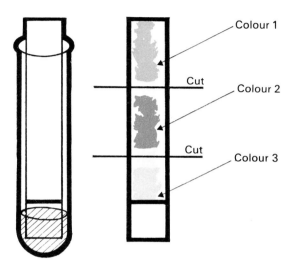

Soak each colour out of the paper with the minimum amount of water.

Mix the separate colours together in different ways to make new colours.

Get some fibre-glass cement filler and follow the directions to fill up a hole in a car body or other object.

Where does glass come from?

How is it made into fibres?

What else is it mixed with in the cement?

What do you have to do to make it set?

What different properties does the final material have from the things which went to make it?

61

What is clay made from?

What can you make from clay?

What happens when you bake clay at a high temperature?

Can you get clay back again?

Try to make clay from pot or brick.

If we make clay into bricks how may we carry the synthesising process further?

Examine plywood, chipboard and blockboard and perhaps try to construct some for yourself. (See *Working with wood Stages 1 and 2.*)

How does their weight, strength, etc, compare with natural woods?

Compare the breaking strength of strips of deal cut along the grain and across the grain and then try a piece of plywood the same size. Does it matter which way you cut the plywood?

Remarkable things have been made by first of all sorting and separating out and then building up the parts to suit our purposes. One of the most interesting things we can do is actually to sort out molecules and then to join them together in different ways to synthesise new chemicals which never existed before. So we can search for and make new substances which have properties we need instead of relying on 'natural' ones.

One branch of this activity produces all our plastics. This might be the point at which to make use of the *Children and plastics* Unit.

The most astonishing example of the natural synthesis of new materials takes place in sexual reproduction. In a most remarkable way the assortment of genes in each sex cell sorts itself out and recombines in the new individual to give a completely different set of characteristics.

If we reproduced asexually we should all look alike and behave in a similar way.

Vive la difference!

9 What about Objectives?

An analysis of the list of Objectives which is reproduced at the back of this Unit will reveal what a very large percentage of them will inevitably be involved in the work suggested. Perhaps the most particularly relevant of them are listed below.

Attitudes, interests and aesthetic awareness
1.04, 1.05, 1.11, 1.12, 1.13, 1.14
2.05, 2.09
3.04, 3.06, 3.07, 3.08, 3.09, 3.12

Observing, exploring and ordering observations
1.21, 1.23, 1.24, 1.25, 1.29a
2.22, 2.23, 2.25
3.21, 3.23

Developing basic concepts and logical thinking
1.32, 1.35
2.33
3.34

Posing questions and devising investigations to answer them
1.42, 1.43
2.42, 2.44, 2.45
3.43

Acquiring knowledge and learning skills
1.51, 1.52, 1.53, 1.54, 1.59, 1.63
2.56, 2.57, 2.58
3.54, 3.56, 3.61, 3.64

Communicating
1.73, 1.76
2.73
3.71

Appreciating patterns and relationships
1.83
2.81, 2.86
3.86

Interpreting findings critically
1.92
2.91, 2.92, 2.93
3.93, 3.95

10 Apparatus and materials

Books

Cherrington, E., *Exploring the Moon through Binoculars,* Peter Davies.
Forsyth, W. S., *Common British Sea Shells,* A. and C. Black.
Hooke, Robert, *Micrographia* (facsimile edition), Dover Publications.
Martin, C. N., *13 Steps to the Atom,* Harrap.
Tebble, N., *British Bivalve Sea Shells,* British Museum (Natural History).
Nuffield Combined Science, *Teachers Guides I, II and III,* Longman and Penguin.

Records

British Bird Series, Shell.
Seven 7-in records of bird songs from Discourses Ltd, 10 High Street, Tunbridge Wells, Kent.

Materials

It is quite impossible to make a comprehensive list of everything which will be needed even if work follows the text closely (which is unlikely). For example, a group may one day need samples of different brands of butter and margarine or a beetroot and a red cabbage. Advice here would be to plan regularly a few days ahead of needs. Growing plants and small animals are called for at times.

Materials to collect
Different kinds of wood, metal, plastics, cloth, rock, paper, card, pebbles, shells, seeds, screws, nails, expanded polystyrene, glass, pottery, rubber.

An assortment of beakers, jugs, bowls, dishes, jars, pans, spoons, plant pots, bottles, screwdrivers, spanners, some of them in sets according to size.

Different kinds of soil (dry), strings and wires.

Common objects in the shape of discs, rings, cylinders, spheres.

A set of blocks of different woods each with the same measurements.

A set of equal-sized strips of several metals and alloys.

An old frying pan (large, without a handle).

Aluminium foil plates and dishes.

Materials commonly found in schools
Modelling clay; plywood; chipboard; powder colour and brushes; paper: plain, coloured, graph, blotting; drinking straws; protractors; chime bars or xylophone, and other musical instruments; magnets.

Materials easily obtained locally
Kitchen powders and liquids, disposable spoons, medical tongue depressors or lollipop sticks, putty, wax, a torch, handbag mirrors.

Batteries: 6 V, 4·5 V (eg Ever-Ready 126), 3 V and 1·5 V (U2).

Bulbs: 1·5 V, 2·5 V, 3·5 V (some 0·15 A and some 0·3 A); and 6 V, 0·06 A.

Bulb-holders, crocodile clips, single bell wire for connecting circuits, some fibre-glass cement filler (used for car-body repairs).

Other apparatus and materials

Displacement cans (home-made).

Measuring cylinders: 100 ml, 250 ml, plastics

Lever arm balance: 250 g/1000 g (eg Nuffield O-Level Physics item 42*).

Spring balances 100 g × 1 g, 200 g × 5 g.

Pocket magnetic compasses.

Hand lenses × 8 or × 10.

A microscope with large depth of focus (eg Offord × 20, from: C. E. Offord, Hurst Green, Etchingham, Sussex; or Bausch and Lomb × 15 binocular microscope).

Micrometer screw gauge, direct reading and Vernier calliper, and plastics models (Osmiroid).

Stop-clock.

Set of metric weights 1 g to 2 kg (slotted weights with a hanger are often very convenient).

Thermometers −10 °C to 110 °C (preferably stirring type).

Clinical thermometer.

Dropping pipettes (medicine droppers).

Specimen tubes (100 × 25 mm) with stoppers.

Universal pH indicator paper.

Filter papers.

Filter funnels.

Items will be found numbered in this way in laboratory suppliers' catalogues, which, if not in primary schools, should be available in Teachers' Centres.

Evaporating dishes.

Conical flasks, 100 ml (Nuffield Chemistry item 585/100). For the distillation apparatus, page 55.

Bung, one hole to fit (Nuffield Chemistry item 549/7). For the distillation apparatus, page 55.

Rubber tubing, 5-mm bore (Nuffield Chemistry item 579). For the distillation apparatus, page 55.

Flexible PVC tubing 5-mm bore (Nuffield Chemistry item 579/6). For the distillation apparatus, page 55.

6-cm, right-angle delivery tubes (Nuffield Chemistry item 210). For the distillation apparatus, page 55.

Test tubes.

Tuning forks.

Wire-wound resistors (5–50 Ω). For these and also for bulbs, wire, etc, try Radiospares, PO Box 427, 13–17 Epworth Street, London EC2P 2HA, if there is difficulty in obtaining them locally.

Alum, copper sulphate, ammonium nitrate, magnesium sulphate (Epsom salts), sodium thiosulphate (hypo).

A safe heat source.

A set of soil sieves. These could very well be home-made. Cut the bases from shallow circular biscuit or toffee tins and replace with perforated zinc or wire gauze of various mesh. About four sieves with holes from about 2 mm downwards are needed. Keep the lids on when shaking.

Ammeter 0–1 A, 0–5 A. Double range (Nuffield item 178).

Voltmeter 0–5 V. 0–15 V. Double range (Nuffield item 179).

Direct reading hygrometer (eg paper hygrometer, Phillip Harris P10443 or Griffin and George S29–102).

Light-meter (as used with cameras).

Tape-recorder.

Binoculars or telescope.

Separating funnel.

Geological hammer.

Chromatography paper.

A small centrifuge.

A much better microscope than either of those mentioned before is a binocular stereo microscope of the 'Sterimag' type. Some schools will have these and full use should be made of them.

As many different kinds of musical instruments as may be borrowed.

Objectives for children learning science
Guide lines to keep in mind

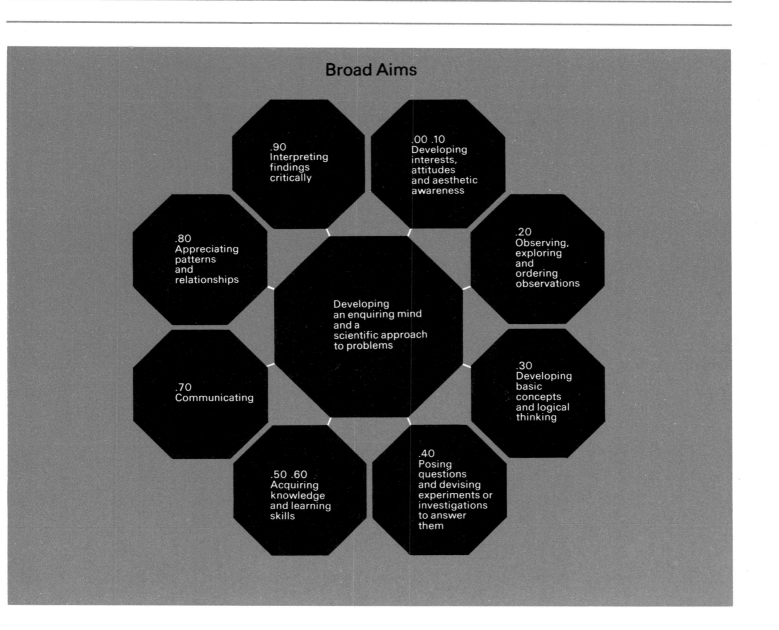

Broad Aims

.90 Interpreting findings critically

.00 .10 Developing interests, attitudes and aesthetic awareness

.80 Appreciating patterns and relationships

.20 Observing, exploring and ordering observations

Developing an enquiring mind and a scientific approach to problems

.70 Communicating

.30 Developing basic concepts and logical thinking

.50 .60 Acquiring knowledge and learning skills

.40 Posing questions and devising experiments or investigations to answer them

Stage 1
Transition from intuition to concrete operations. Infants generally.

The characteristics of thought among infant children differ in important respects from those of children over the age of about seven years. Infant thought has been described as 'intuitive' by Piaget; it is closely associated with physical action and is dominated by immediate observation. Generally, the infant is not able to think about or imagine the consequences of an action unless he has actually carried it out, nor is he yet likely to draw logical conclusions from his experiences. At this early stage the objectives are those concerned with active exploration of the immediate environment and the development of ability to discuss and communicate effectively: they relate to the kind of activities that are appropriate to these very young children, and which form an introduction to ways of exploring and of ordering observations.

1.01 Willingness to ask questions
1.02 Willingness to handle both living and non-living material.
1.03 Sensitivity to the need for giving proper care to living things.
1.04 Enjoyment in using all the senses for exploring and discriminating.
1.05 Willingness to collect material for observation or investigation.

Concrete operations. Early stage.

In this Stage, children are developing the ability to manipulate things mentally. At first this ability is limited to objects and materials that can be manipulated concretely, and even then only in a restricted way. The objectives here are concerned with developing these mental operations through exploration of concrete objects and materials—that is to say, objects and materials which, as physical things, have meaning for the child. Since older children, and even adults prefer an introduction to new ideas and problems through concrete example and physical exploration, these objectives are suitable for all children, whatever their age, who are being introduced to certain science activities for the first time.

1.06 Desire to find out things for oneself.
1.07 Willing participation in group work.
1.08 Willing compliance with safety regulations in handling tools and equipment.
1.09 Appreciation of the need to learn the meaning of new words and to use them correctly.

Stage 2
Concrete operations. Later stage.

In this Stage, a continuation of what Piaget calls the stage of concrete operations, the mental manipulations are becoming more varied and powerful. The developing ability to handle variables—for example, in dealing with multiple classification—means that problems can be solved in more ordered and quantitative ways than was previously possible. The objectives begin to be more specific to the exploration of the scientific aspects of the environment rather than to general experience, as previously. These objectives are developments of those of Stage 1 and depend on them for a foundation. They are those thought of as being appropriate for all children who have progressed from Stage 1 and not merely for nine- to eleven-year-olds.

2.01 Willingness to co-operate with others in science activities.
2.02 Willingness to observe objectively.
2.03 Appreciation of the reasons for safety regulations.
2.04 Enjoyment in examining ambiguity in the use of words.
2.05 Interest in choosing suitable means of expressing results and observations.
2.06 Willingness to assume responsibility for the proper care of living things.
2.07 Willingness to examine critically the results of their own and others' work.
2.08 Preference for putting ideas to test before accepting or rejecting them.
2.09 Appreciation that approximate methods of comparison may be more appropriate than careful measurements.

Stage 3
Transition to stage of abstract thinking.

This is the Stage in which, for some children, the ability to think about abstractions is developing. When this development is complete their thought is capable of dealing with the possible and hypothetical, and is not tied to the concrete and to the here and now. It may take place between eleven and thirteen for some able children, for some children it may happen later, and for others it may never occur. The objectives of this stage are ones which involve development of ability to use hypothetical reasoning and to separate and combine variables in a systematic way. They are appropriate to those who have achieved most of the Stage 2 objectives and who now show signs of ability to manipulate mentally ideas and propositions.

3.01 Acceptance of responsibility for their own and others' safety in experiments.
3.02 Preference for using words correctly.
3.03 Commitment to the idea of physical cause and effect.
3.04 Recognition of the need to standardise measurements.
3.05 Willingness to examine evidence critically.
3.06 Willingness to consider beforehand the usefulness of the results from a possible experiment.
3.07 Preference for choosing the most appropriate means of expressing results or observations.
3.08 Recognition of the need to acquire new skills.
3.09 Willingness to consider the role of science in everyday life.

Attitudes, interests and aesthetic awareness

.00/.10

Observing, exploring and ordering observations

.20

1.21 Appreciation of the variety of living things and materials in the environment.
1.22 Awareness of changes which take place as time passes.
1.23 Recognition of common shapes—square, circle, triangle.
1.24 Recognition of regularity in patterns.
1.25 Ability to group things consistently according to chosen or given criteria.

1.11 Awareness that there are various ways of testing out ideas and making observations.
1.12 Interest in comparing and classifying living or non-living things.
1.13 Enjoyment in comparing measurements with estimates.
1.14 Awareness that there are various ways of expressing results and observations.
1.15 Willingness to wait and to keep records in order to observe change in things.
1.16 Enjoyment in exploring the variety of living things in the environment.
1.17 Interest in discussing and comparing the aesthetic qualities of materials.

1.26 Awareness of the structure and form of living things.
1.27 Awareness of change of living things and non-living materials.
1.28 Recognition of the action of force
1.29 Ability to group living and non-living things by observable attributes.
1.29a Ability to distinguish regularity in events and motion.

2.11 Enjoyment in developing methods for solving problems or testing ideas.
2.12 Appreciation of the part that aesthetic qualities of materials play in determining their use.
2.13 Interest in the way discoveries were made in the past.

2.21 Awareness of internal structure in living and non-living things.
2.22 Ability to construct and use keys for identification.
2.23 Recognition of similar and congruent shapes.
2.24 Awareness of symmetry in shapes and structures.
2.25 Ability to classify living things and non-living materials in different ways.
2.26 Ability to visualise objects from different angles and the shape of cross-sections.

3.11 Appreciation of the main principles in the care of living things.
3.12 Willingness to extend methods used in science activities to other fields of experience.

3.21 Appreciation that classification criteria are arbitrary.
3.22 Ability to distinguish observations which are relevant to the solution of a problem from those which are not.
3.23 Ability to estimate the order of magnitude of physical quantities.

69

Developing basic concepts and logical thinking .30	Posing questions and devising experiments or investigations to answer them .40

Stage 1
Transition from intuition to concrete operations. Infants generally.

1.31 Awareness of the meaning of words which describe various types of quantity.
1.32 Appreciation that things which are different may have features in common.

1.41 Ability to find answers to simple problems by investigation
1.42 Ability to make comparisons in terms of one property or variable.

- -

Concrete operations. Early stage.

1.33 Ability to predict the effect of certain changes through observation of similar changes.
1.34 Formation of the notions of the horizontal and the vertical.
1.35 Development of concepts of conservation of length and substance.
1.36 Awareness of the meaning of speed and of its relation to distance covered.

1.43 Appreciation of the need for measurement.
1.44 Awareness that more than one variable may be involved in a particular change.

Stage 2
Concrete operations. Later stage.

2.31 Appreciation of measurement as division into regular parts and repeated comparison with a unit.
2.32 Appreciation that comparisons can be made indirectly by use of an intermediary.
2.33 Development of concepts of conservation of weight, area and volume.
2.34 Appreciation of weight as a downward force.
2.35 Understanding of the speed, time, distance relation.

2.41 Ability to frame questions likely to be answered through investigations.
2.42 Ability to investigate variables and to discover effective ones.
2.43 Appreciation of the need to control variables and use controls in investigations.
2.44 Ability to choose and use either arbitrary or standard units of measurement as appropriate.
2.45 Ability to select a suitable degree of approximation and work to it.
2.46 Ability to use representational models for investigating problems or relationships.

Stage 3
Transition to stage of abstract thinking.

3.31 Familiarity with relationships involving velocity, distance, time, acceleration.
3.32 Ability to separate, exclude or combine variables in approaching problems.
3.33 Ability to formulate hypotheses not dependent upon direct observation.
3.34 Ability to extend reasoning beyond the actual to the possible.
3.35 Ability to distinguish a logically sound proof from others less sound.

3.41 Attempting to identify the essential steps in approaching a problem scientifically.
3.42 Ability to design experiments with effective controls for testing hypotheses.
3.43 Ability to visualise a hypothetical situation as a useful simplification of actual observations.
3.44 Ability to construct scale models for investigation and to appreciate implications of changing the scale.

70

1.51 Ability to discriminate between different materials.
1.52 Awareness of the characteristics of living things.
1.53 Awareness of properties which materials can have.
1.54 Ability to use displayed reference material for identifying living and non-living things.

1.55 Familiarity with sources of sound.
1.56 Awareness of sources of heat, light and electricity.
1.57 Knowledge that change can be produced in common substances.
1.58 Appreciation that ability to move or cause movement requires energy.
1.59 Knowledge of differences in properties between and within common groups of materials.

1.61 Appreciation of man's use of other living things and their products.
1.62 Awareness that man's way of life has changed through the ages.
1.63 Skill in manipulating tools and materials.
1.64 Development of techniques for handling living things correctly.
1.65 Ability to use books for supplementing ideas or information.

2.51 Knowledge of conditions which promote changes in living things and non-living materials.
2.52 Familiarity with a wide range of forces and of ways in which they can be changed.
2.53 Knowledge of sources and simple properties of common forms of energy.
2.54 Knowledge of the origins of common materials.
2.55 Awareness of some discoveries and inventions by famous scientists.
2.56 Knowledge of ways to investigate and measure properties of living things and non-living materials.
2.57 Awareness of changes in the design of measuring instruments and tools during man's history.
2.58 Skill in devising and constructing simple apparatus.
2.59 Ability to select relevant information from books or other reference material.

3.51 Knowledge that chemical change results from interaction.
3.52 Knowledge that energy can be stored and converted in various ways.
3.53 Awareness of the universal nature of gravity.
3.54 Knowledge of the main constituents and variations in the composition of soil and of the earth.
3.55 Knowledge that properties of matter can be explained by reference to its particulate nature.
3.56 Knowledge of certain properties of heat, light, sound, electrical, mechanical and chemical energy.
3.57 Knowledge of a wide range of living organisms.
3.58 Development of the concept of an internal environment.
3.59 Knowledge of the nature and variations in basic life processes.

3.61 Appreciation of levels of organisation in living things.
3.62 Appreciation of the significance of the work and ideas of some famous scientists.
3.63 Ability to apply relevant knowledge without help of contextual cues.
3.64 Ability to use scientific equipment and instruments for extending the range of human senses.

71

Communicating	Appreciating patterns and relationships
.70	**.80**

Stage 1
Transition from intuition to concrete operations. Infants generally.

1.71 Ability to use new words appropriately.
1.72 Ability to record events in their sequences.
1.73 Ability to discuss and record impressions of living and non-living things in the environment.
1.74 Ability to use representational symbols for recording information on charts or block graphs.

1.81 Awareness of cause-effect relationships.

Concrete operations. Early stage.

1.75 Ability to tabulate information and use tables.
1.76 Familiarity with names of living things and non-living materials.
1.77 Ability to record impressions by making models, painting or drawing.

1.82 Development of a concept of environment.
1.83 Formation of a broad idea of variation in living things.
1.84 Awareness of seasonal changes in living things.
1.85 Awareness of differences in physical conditions between different parts of the Earth.

Stage 2
Concrete operations. Later stage.

2.71 Ability to use non-representational symbols in plans, charts, etc.
2.72 Ability to interpret observations in terms of trends and rates of change.
2.73 Ability to use histograms and other simple graphical forms for communicating data.
2.74 Ability to construct models as a means of recording observations.

2.81 Awareness of sequences of change in natural phenomena.
2.82 Awareness of structure-function relationship in parts of living things.
2.83 Appreciation of interdependence among living things.
2.84 Awareness of the impact of man's activities on other living things.
2.85 Awareness of the changes in the physical environment brought about by man's activity.
2.86 Appreciation of the relationships of parts and wholes.

Stage 3
Transition to stage of abstract thinking.

3.71 Ability to select the graphical form most appropriate to the information being recorded.
3.72 Ability to use three-dimensional models or graphs for recording results.
3.73 Ability to deduce information from graphs: from gradient, area, intercept.
3.74 Ability to use analogies to explain scientific ideas and theories.

3.81 Recognition that the ratio of volume to surface area is significant.
3.82 Appreciation of the scale of the universe.
3.83 Understanding of the nature and significance of changes in living and non-living things.
3.84 Recognition that energy has many forms and is conserved when it is changed from one form to another.
3.85 Recognition of man's impact on living things—conservation, change, control.
3.86 Appreciation of the social implications of man's changing use of materials, historical and contemporary.
3.87 Appreciation of the social implications of research in science.
3.88 Appreciation of the role of science in the changing pattern of provision for human needs.

Interpreting findings critically

.91   Awareness that the apparent size, shape and relationships of things depend on the position of the observer.

- -

1.92   Appreciation that properties of materials influence their use.

These Stages we have chosen conform to modern ideas about children's learning. They conveniently describe for us the mental development of children between the ages of five and thirteen years, but it must be remembered that ALTHOUGH CHILDREN GO THROUGH THESE STAGES IN THE SAME ORDER THEY DO NOT GO THROUGH THEM AT THE SAME RATES .
SOME children achieve the later Stages at an early age.
SOME loiter in the early Stages for quite a time.
SOME never have the mental ability to develop to the later Stages.
ALL appear to be ragged in their movement from one Stage to another.
Our Stages, then, are not tied to chronological age, so in any one class of children there will be, almost certainly, some children at differing Stages of mental development.

2.91   Appreciation of adaptation to environment.
2.92   Appreciation of how the form and structure of materials relate to their function and properties.
2.93   Awareness that many factors need to be considered when choosing a material for a particular use.
2.94   Recognition of the role of chance in making measurements and experiments.

3.91   Ability to draw from observations conclusions that are unbiased by preconception.
3.92   Willingness to accept factual evidence despite preceptual contradictions.
3.93   Awareness that the degree of accuracy of measurements has to be taken into account when results are interpreted.
3.94   Awareness that unstated assumptions can affect conclusions drawn from argument or experimental results.
3.95   Appreciation of the need to integrate findings into a simplifying generalisation.
3.96   Willingness to check that conclusions are consistent with further evidence.

Index

Illustration acknowledgements:

The publishers gratefully acknowledge the help given by the following in supplying photographs on the pages indicated:

Australian News and Information Bureau, 54
Bruce Coleman Limited, 40, 41 top
Cambridge Scientific Instruments Limited, 24, 25
Commissioner of Police of the Metropolis, 39
Dover Publications, Inc., 22
Dutch Dairy Bureau, 34
Frank Lane, 41
Glass Manufacturers Federation, 35
Gliksten Doors, 38
Government of India Tourist Office, 44
Phototheque l'Express, 37
Post Office, 3
Quo'tass (photographers) Limited, 26, 29
Science Museum, 55
Shell Photographic Service, 2
United Feature Syndicate, Inc., 4

Line drawings by Sandy Rawlinson and Russell Springham

Cover design by Peter Gauld